SEED FOR THE SOWER

Seed for the Sower

Preaching Matters

Alexander Goussetis

HOLY CROSS ORTHODOX PRESS
Brookline, Massachusetts

© 2011 Holy Cross Orthodox Press
Published by Holy Cross Orthodox Press
50 Goddard Avenue
Brookline, Massachusetts 02445

ISBN-13 978-1-935317-20-3
ISBN-10 1-935317-20-2

Library of Congress Cataloging-in-Publication Data
Goussetis, Alexander.
 Seed for the sower : preaching matters / Alexander Goussetis.
  p. cm.
 Includes bibliographical references (p.   ).
 ISBN-13: 978-1-935317-20-3
 ISBN-10: 1-935317-20-2
 1. Orthodox Eastern Church--Sermons. 2. Preaching--History--Early church, ca. 30-600. I. Title.
 BX330.G68 2011
 252'.019--dc22
                                              2011007501

To Rev. Thomas FitzGerald, Rev. Alexander Cutler,
and Rev. Nicholas Palis—spiritual fathers
who have guided me during different periods of my life.

CONTENTS

PART II
SELECTED SERMONS

PREFACE

Let anyone with ears listen!
(Matt 11:15)

Entering an Orthodox Church for worship directly impacts the senses. Whether one gazes meditatively at an icon, venerates a holy relic, tastes the mystical Eucharist, or draws in the fragrance of incense, the senses invite the presence of God. The same is true with the gift of listening, especially when hearing the saving message of the gospel.

The role of preaching in the Church is not an appendix to the actual worship service itself, but an integral part of the proclamation of the faith. Orthodoxy does not relegate homiletics to second-class status, but rather views this *charisma* as an opportunity to connect life with faith for the believers. This fact is verified in the history of the Church. For this reason, I have chosen to divide the contents of this book into two sections. Part I offers a brief historical survey of the role of preaching in the Church. Part II presents practical examples of a contemporary homiletic style.

This book is offered for consideration with two audiences in mind. First is the preacher. My hope is that the homilist will find a notion or idea to use as a springboard for developing a sermon. The second audience for this book is the Christian who uses these messages for spiritual reading.

An important caveat must be expressed from the outset. All of the homilies that follow were sparked by thoughts or insights from others that I formed into my own message. I am acutely aware that I stand on the shoulders of others. If there is a specific reference, illustration, or quotation that I have borrowed without due credit, please accept my apologies. Having stated that, I invite you, the reader, to use, copy, change, and borrow freely what you find here for your own homiletic discourses.

Before closing, I wish to express my deepest gratitude to Dr. Anton Vrame for his guidance throughout this project. As with my three other published books, Dr. Vrame offered his technical and stylistic expertise on this manuscript. He combines a great intellectual capacity together with an eye for the practical. May our Lord Jesus Christ continue to bless and sanctify his ministry.

Gabriela Fulton proved a valuable resource for this project. Her technical support and editing were essential components that added greatly to the finished product.

Also deserving of acknowledgement is Presbytera Lisa Goussetis, who was a sounding board for many of these messages. Her knowledge of the faith, coupled with a flair for English composition, proved vital to the construction and editing of these sermons.

Finally, I would be remiss if I didn't extend my appreciation to the congregations that first received these messages. Their feedback over the years has been, and continues to be, an effective tool in honing my preaching skills.

PART I

DEVELOPMENT OF PREACHING
IN THE ORTHODOX CHURCH

Preach the word, be urgent in season and out of season;
convince, rebuke, and exhort, be unfailing in patience
and in teaching.

(2 Tim 4:2)

The gift of preaching has been an integral part of the pathway to salvation from the earliest days of the Christian Church. A preacher is a κῆρυξ, a "divine herald," a term used more than sixty times in the New Testament. Preachers are proclaimers of the kingdom, messengers of the divine gospel of Jesus Christ. Preachers are teachers of eternal truth. Preachers are witnesses (μάρτυρες) to the message of God, even to the point of martyrdom.

Those who preach fulfill a variety of pastoral roles, such as persuading, showing, living, comforting, reproving, strengthening, and inspiring the flock.[1] In addition, preachers teach the content of the Christian faith and interpret the tradition of the Church, including Scripture, in light of the contemporary situation of their flocks. They strive to discern the "signs of the times" and point to signs of God's presence in the lives of their congregations. Preaching is not mere public expression of opinion, but an urgent eschatological activity.

When we consider the historical development and role of preaching in the context of the Orthodox Church, significant questions arise: Who were the first preachers? What did they preach about, and what methods did they use? What issues were uppermost in their minds, and how did they relate to the world around them? What part does God play, and what part does the preacher play, in the proclamation of the gospel?[2]

PENTECOST AND THE FIRST PREACHERS

Following the dramatic descent of the Holy Spirit on the day of Pentecost, the Apostle Peter offered the first sermon in the history of the Church. The second chapter of the book of Acts informs us that three thousand people were baptized and brought into the Church following Peter's message. The fourth chapter highlights that five thousand new Christians were welcomed into the faith through Peter's vibrant proclamation of the gospel.

The impact of the primitive preaching of Peter and the other apostles was remarkable. The first preachers enjoyed neither the approval of the powerful Roman imperial authorities, nor the Judaic hierarchy, nor even the educated citizens of the empire. They faced hostilities at every turn. Yet despite these obstacles, the gospel spread.[3]

Initially the converts to this new religious establishment were members of the Jewish Diaspora, but eventually the gospel attracted a wider Gentile interest. As the budding communities grew, new problems became apparent. The congregations' theology, which had not yet been fully elaborated, made them easy prey to misinformation or distortion of the faith. Similarly, preachers and other converts suffered from continual pressure from family and friends to revert to their former ways and beliefs. The temptation to apostatize was great, and it became clear that, together with evangelization, education was increasingly more necessary.[4]

With the dramatic conversion of Paul of Tarsus came not only a person with missionary zeal, but an educated pastor who could mold and shape Christian communities. Congregations were now so widely dispersed that the missionary preachers could no longer give them personal supervision, so Paul developed the next dimension of preaching—the epistolary sermon.

In sending his spoken word to the communities, Paul claimed the same authority as if he were actually present. As he wrote, "For though absent in body, I am present in spirit" (1 Cor 5:3). By means of letters, he continued to guide congregations from afar. Paul intended to send his messages in order to correct potentially heretical teachings.

From a pastoral perspective, we see that Paul addressed each congregation according to its distinct situation and circumstance, while proclaiming one basic message. He preached to budding communities as a pastor who was interested in building up the body of Christ, as each church struggled with its unique circumstances. His basic message is oneness; all believers are baptized into this one body:[5] "For just as the body is one and has many members, and all the members of the body, though many, are one body, so it is with Christ" (1 Cor 12:12–13).

Paul constantly battles against those who corrupt the gospel message and lead people into apostasy. His approach is primarily centered in conceptual argument, not in narratives, which dominate the preaching of Jesus.[6] Paul rarely makes use of the life and ministry of Jesus in his writings. Instead he offers practical counsels to strengthen the congregations and equip them to win others for the faith. The overall preaching model that evolves from Paul's letters is summed up in two words, *Christology* and *ethics*: learn the faith, and live the faith daily.

THE APOSTOLIC PERIOD

By the end of the first and beginning of the second century, the foundational voices of the apostles had died off. Whereas it had once been possible to settle disagreements by calling an apostolic council in Jerusalem or seeking the guidance of a recognized figure such as James or Paul, the Church now experienced the loss of authority figures of sufficient stature to arbitrate disputes.[7] A void needed to be filled to guide the fledgling Church through this transitional post-apostolic stage.

Soon a diverse group, including Clement of Rome, Ignatius of Antioch, and Polycarp of Smyrna, surfaced to provide leadership and stability. These Fathers' writings, if not actually called homilies, were homiletic in form and designed for public reading. Their messages, for the most part, were not intended to systematize the dogmatic positions of the Christian faith. Rather, the preachers of this era addressed the role of the Church as a safe haven and trusted guide to one's life and salvation.

For example, Clement dealt with factions that threatened the unity of the Corinthian community, not unlike Paul during his ministry:

> We acknowledge that we have been somewhat slow in giving attention to the matters in dispute among you, dear friends, especially the detestable and unholy schism, so alien and strange to those chosen by God, which a few reckless and arrogant persons

have kindled to such a pitch of insanity that your good name, once so renowned and loved by all, has been greatly reviled.[8]

Ignatius continued developing this theme of unity in Christ through the Church by encouraging the faithful to meet frequently, even in the face of hostile forces. He exhorted the faithful in Magnesia on the need for spiritual leadership and mutual accountability required in the body of Christ:

> Be eager, therefore, to be firmly grounded in the precepts of the Lord and the apostles, in order that in whatever you do, you may prosper, physically and spiritually, in faith and love, in the Son and the Father and in the Spirit . . . Be subject to the bishop and to one another, as Jesus Christ in the flesh was to the Father, and as the apostles were to Christ and to the Father, that there may be unity, both physical and spiritual.[9]

With such enmity hovering over the life of the faithful, the preachers of this era often commented on the threat of martyrdom that faced every Christian. Ignatius was taken prisoner during a persecution of the Church in Antioch. He was placed in chains and escorted, along with others, by a unit of soldiers to Rome. For Ignatius, Christ's Passion, death, and Resurrection were proof of eternal life in the risen Christ. Ignatius believed that, had Christ died only in appearance, his own suffering and his readiness to sacrifice his life for Christ would have no meaning. Ignatius's preaching focused on the blessedness of those who persevere to the end, and he graphically described what awaited himself at his own martyrdom:

> Fire and cross and battles with wild beasts, mutilation, mangling, wrenching of bones, the hacking of limbs, the crushing of my whole body, cruel tortures of the devil—let these come upon me, only let me reach Jesus Christ![10]

In summary, the Apostolic Fathers offered reassurance, strength of faith, and their own lives as witnesses to their preaching. They sought a new identity for the body of the Church, free of Jewish and Roman influences. The anonymous author of the *Epistle to Diognetus* eloquently painted an image of the distinctiveness of the Christian in the midst of a harsh and dangerous world:

> They live in their own countries, but only as nonresidents; they participate in everything as citizens, and endure everything as

foreigners. Every foreign country is their fatherland, and every fatherland is foreign . . . They are in the flesh, but do not live according to the flesh. They live on earth, but their citizenship is in heaven.[11]

THE APOLOGISTS

As the Church grew, Christians began to be more noticed and their teachings and practices attacked. In the second and third centuries, the Church defended itself against the religious, social, and political forces of the Roman Empire. Christians were viewed suspiciously as people who practiced ritual murder, cannibalism, incest, and magic. Such sensational attitudes were difficult to dislodge. Even divisions within the Church threatened the unity of the flock, with the heretical teachings of Gnosticism and Marcionism being propagated.

Against this backdrop emerged a host of Christian defenders who produced a new style of preaching for the Church. This august group included Irenaeus of Lyons, Justin Martyr, Clement of Alexandria, Tertullian, and Origen of Alexandria. The list of critics who challenged these preachers spanned the spectrum. To pagan Rome, the Christians were considered atheists, disloyal to the state. To Greek philosophers, Christians were viewed as weak in substantive thought. To the Jews, the Christians' belief in a crucified God was scandalous.

To the charge of atheism, Justin clearly stated that his preaching was grounded in the Trinitarian God:

Thus are we even called atheists. We do proclaim ourselves atheists as regards those whom you call gods, but not with respect to the Most High God, who is alien to all evil and is the Father of justice, temperance, and the other virtues. We revere and worship Him and the Son who came forth from Him and taught us these things . . . and the Prophetic Spirit, and we pay homage to them.[12]

The Apologists spoke primarily for the edification of their Christian audiences. Yet they also felt compelled to address the philosophical and intellectual voices of the day. Trained in the ways of the academic elite, the Apologists aimed to respond to the philosophers on their own grounds.[13] Their work is the first attempt at reconciling reason and revelation. In that light, Justin defended the truth of Christ's teachings with the following statement:

> Beyond doubt, our teachings are more noble than all human teaching, because Christ, who appeared on earth for our sakes, became the whole Logos, namely Logos and body and soul. Everything that the philosophers and legislators discovered and expressed well, they accomplished through their discovery and contemplation of some part of the Logos. But since they did not have a full knowledge of the Logos, which is Christ, they often contradicted themselves.[14]

The term *Gnosticism* is derived from the Greek word for "knowledge." This philosophy did not center on learning truths about the human and natural world through reason. Rather, it taught that "revealed knowledge" became available only to those who received the secret teachings of a heavenly revealer. Clement of Alexandria, who was deeply rooted in philosophy, was a firm advocate of the basic harmony between faith and knowledge. Yet he scolded those Gnostics who claimed a higher standing than other Christians:

> It is a matter of wonder to me that some people dare to call themselves perfect and Gnostics, laying claim in their inflated pride to a loftier state than the Apostle. Paul himself made only this claim: "Not that I have already claimed this, or already been made perfect, but I press on hoping that I may lay hold of that which Jesus Christ has laid hold of me. But one thing I do: forgetting what is behind, I strain forward to what is before, I press on toward the goal, to the prize of God's heavenly call in Christ Jesus" (Philippians 3:12–14). He considers himself perfect in the sense that he has changed his old way of life and follows a better one, but not in the sense that he is perfect in knowledge, rather that he only desires what is perfect.[15]

The Apologists built their case around the goodness of the Creator, the universality of reason and law, and the perfection of all things in Christ. This love of truth enabled Christians to pursue honest dialogue, wherever it may lead. This blueprint for combating worldly ideologies with the gospel continues to the present day.

THE GOLDEN AGE OF PREACHING

The conversion of Emperor Constantine to Christianity in the early fourth century opened a new era in the life of the Church and in the art of preaching. Dramatic changes in congregational life emerged as catacombs were replaced with spacious cathedrals. The liturgical life of the faithful became more sophisticated with the celebration of various festivals of saints and martyrs, increasing the need for thematic preaching and panegyrics.

From this "Golden Age" emerged a cluster of great theologians: Basil the Great, Gregory the Theologian, and John Chrysostom. Highly educated, these eminent Fathers fine-tuned Trinitarian doctrine, led the fight against Arianism, spread monastic discipline throughout the empire, and were excellent preachers and hierarchs. Their homiletical literature constitutes one of the Church's richest legacies, providing an eloquent testimony to the pastoral effect of these spiritual shepherds. Among their many gifts was the ability to make accessible to the ordinary faithful the supernatural truths of revelation: "They tried to be faithful to the sublime nature of the spoken Word of God, without diminishing the divine mystery, difficult as this may be to anyone who attempts to bring revelation closer to human understanding."[16]

The Pastoral and Preaching Presence of Basil the Great

St. Basil was the product of a wealthy and distinguished family. Although his father was responsible for encouraging him in intellectual pursuits, his religious formation was greatly influenced by his grandmother, Macrina the Elder. Basil was first educated in Caesarea and later in Constantinople and Athens. Although gifted in academic disciplines, Basil was drawn to the monastic life, journeying through Syria and Egypt to study the life of the monks of those regions. He returned home, distributed his goods to the poor, and began a life devoted to God. Basil and his friend Gregory (the Theologian) formed a rule for monasteries in the Pontic desert, and these writings influenced monasticism for centuries.

In 364 Basil was ordained to the priesthood and served as an advisor to Eusebius, bishop of Caesarea. When Eusebius died in 370, Basil succeeded him as hierarch. He found many abuses to be corrected, including simony, and encountered a good deal of opposition to his reforms. He gained the trust of his new flock with a combination of pastoral love, eloquence, and charity. Basil strove for one goal throughout the course of his pastorate: to gather together the divided forces of the Church in order to oppose heresy with a strong and organized body, united by strength of faith and purpose.[17]

The breadth of Basil's extensive literature included works on dogmatic theology, exegetical writings, ascetical rules, letters, and homilies. His gift as a pastor and orator was the ability to communicate inscrutable truths of the Church in ways that both lay and clergy could benefit from. A classic example is his elaboration on the mystery of the Holy Spirit:

> Through the Holy Spirit comes our restoration to Paradise, our ascension to the Kingdom of heaven, our adoption as God's children, our freedom to call God our Father, our becoming partakers of the grace of Christ, being called children of light, sharing in eternal glory, and in a word, our inheritance of the fullness of blessing, both in this world and the world to come.[18]

In many of his writings, Basil is concerned with the role of the preacher:

> In *Moral Rule 70*, for example, Basil says the contents of the message must be exemplified in his own life: "The leader must himself possess what he brings" and "one must not put constraint upon others to do what he has not done himself." Finally, "the leader of the word should make himself an example to others of every good thing, practicing first what he preaches.[19]

On the proclamation itself, in his *Moral Rule 70*, Basil warns of some impediments to preaching:

1. The preacher must not flatter the hearers, satisfying their own pleasures.
2. He must not abuse his authority either to insult them or exalt himself over them.
3. He must not imagine that he himself is credited with preaching, but that he is a "co-worker" (συνεργοὶ) with the Spirit.
4. He must not put himself at the disposal of those who pay special attention to him, i.e. he must not preach in order to receive "favors."[20]

Basil wrote a series of homilies on the book of Psalms that combined exegetical analysis with practical application. He manifested his intense devotion to the Holy Scriptures through these sermons and attempted to awaken a similar reverence in his flock. He encouraged his readers to cull wisdom from the pages of this book of prayer:

> Now, the prophets teach one thing, historians another, the law something else, and the form of advice found in the proverbs something different still. But, the Book of Psalms has taken over what is profitable from all. It foretells coming events; it recalls history; it frames laws for life; it suggests what must be done; and in general, it is the common treasury of good doctrine, carefully finding what is suitable for each one.[21]

Basil lived during a time when persecutions were past, but when theological debates brought forth challenges, and sometimes confusion, for the Christian faithful. During his era the Church sought solid ground amidst the influence of meddling emperors and ambitious hierarchs. In his life and pastorate, Basil tried "with a striking degree of success to do justice to the claims of unity and truth, of richness and order, of faith and culture, and of theology and life."[22]

The Pastoral and Preaching Presence of Gregory the Theologian

Gregory was born in the obscure town of Arianzum (near Nazianzus) around the year 330. By all accounts, this area in southwest Cappadocia is described as rustic and practically uninhabitable. From his youth, Gregory was enthralled with learning. He received a thorough education in ancient literature, oratory, history, and philosophy in his native Nazianzus, in Caesarea, in Alexandria, and finally in Athens. While in Athens, Gregory began a lifelong friendship with Basil of Caesarea. Gregory remained a perpetual student until age thirty, hoping to avoid public acclaim and positions of influence. However, his father, Gregory the Elder, the bishop of Nazianzus, had other plans for his introspective son. Ordained to the priesthood against his will in 361, Gregory remained in Nazianzus as his father's assistant for almost ten years.

In 372, once again against his will, through the "political" maneuvering of his friend Bishop Basil (who wished to fill the episcopacy with bishops who would defend the faith of Nicea against the ongoing Arian teachings in the empire), Gregory was assigned to the bishopric of Sasima. Beginning his episcopal ministry in a remote area and serving an ignorant and divisive flock, Gregory was indignant toward Basil, preferring instead to live a reflective and peaceful life.

In 379 Gregory left for Constantinople, where he found a Church even more dispirited and tumultuous. "His struggle with the Arians was often violent. He was attacked by murderers, his church was stormed by mobs, he was pelted with stones, and his opponents accused him of brawling and disturbing the peace."[23] Despite all hindrances, Gregory initiated a magnificent preaching ministry, especially notable for the Five Theological Orations. These sermons focus on the nature of God and on the doctrine of the Trinity and are considered among the most outstanding examples of Christian eloquence.

Amidst this upheaval, Gregory was soon installed as archbishop of Constantinople. His frustration, however, at the Second Ecumenical Council in 381 led Gregory to resign his position, whereupon he returned to administer his father's church in Nazianzus. Not long after, Gregory retired to a life of writing and traveling to monasteries, fatigued by the demands of Church life.

As brilliant a theologian as Gregory is recognized to be, we might conclude that his contributions to the Church were solely intellectual. That perspective, however, would not account for his creativeness in espousing new theological positions and using models that were both new and influential.[24] An expression of his stylistic beauty is this masterpiece in another of his momentous orations, on the paradoxes of Jesus:

> He was born, but he was already begotten; he issued from a woman, but she was a virgin . . . He was wrapped in swaddling bands, but he removed the swaddling clothes of the grave when he arose again. He was laid in a manger, but he was glorified by angels, and proclaimed by a star, and worshipped by the Magi . . . On the mountain he was bright as the lightening, and became more luminous than the sun . . .
>
> He was baptized as man, but he remitted sins as God. He hungered, but he fed thousands. He thirsted, but he cried, "If any man thirsts, let him come unto me and drink." He was weary, but he is the peace of them that are sorrowful and heavy-laden.
>
> He prays, but he hears prayers. He weeps, but he puts an end to tears. He asks where Lazarus was laid, for he was a man;

and he raises Lazarus, for he is God . . . As a sheep he is led to the slaughter, but he is the Shepherd of Israel and now of the whole world . . . He is bruised and wounded, but he heals every disease and every infirmity. He is lifted up and nailed to the tree, but by the tree of life he restores us . . . He lays down his life, but he has the power to take it again . . . He dies, but gives life, and by his death he destroys death. He is buried, but he rises again.[25]

Gregory's *Apologia* is another of his memorable sermons. In this series of messages, Gregory highlighted the burdens of priesthood, insisting that the priest-servant must be a living and holy sacrifice to God:

A man must himself be cleansed before cleansing others; himself become wise, that he may make others wise; become light, before he can give light; draw near to God before he can bring others near; be hallowed, before he can hallow them; be possessed of hands before leading others by the hand; and of wisdom before he can speak wisely.[26]

Gregory's gift of language lifted his sermons to unparalleled heights. His messages offered during feast days, his funeral orations—important for the historical material they contain—and his *Last Farewell*, offered in 381, remain significant prototypes of preaching genius.

The Pastoral and Preaching Presence of John Chrysostom

Born to a prominent and aristocratic family around the year 347, John the "Golden Mouth" (*Chrysostomos*) was the preeminent evangelist and preacher of his era, and many Christians—both Eastern and Western—still regard him as the preeminent example of a homilist. Not a theologian or philosopher in the classical sense, he instead used contemporary issues of the day to teach and expound on moral imperatives.

He began his formative years as an ascetic, following the death of his mother. After a short novitiate, he returned to the world and was ordained a deacon in 381 and a priest in 386. Chrysostom discussed his calling in the famous six books *On the Priesthood*. He described the highest duty of his office as the performance of the sacraments. He added that this sacred role included the priest as a teacher, mentor, preacher, and pastor of souls. In 398 Chrysostom was elevated to the episcopacy of the see of Constantinople.

Much of contemporary preaching involves perception and presentation: attractive and well-dressed speakers, elaborate stages, professional sound systems and visual screens, and an audience ready to be entertained. John Chrysostom would fail miserably in our present era. His physique was "small and emaciated"; he had a "huge, bald head and straggly beard."[27] His voice was neither loud nor sweet sounding and, in order to be heard, he often left his episcopal throne, which was located in the rear of the altar, to preach extemporaneously from the *ambo*, a platform usually situated in front of the altar and closer to the congregation.[28] His style of preaching was "blunt-spoken, ill-tempered and harsh."[29] Yet his method of delivery both charmed and transfixed the masses, with his profound sermons exciting readers even to the present day.

From a preacher's perspective, Chrysostom clearly understood the difference between an essay or any other text, which is read, and a sermon, which is delivered. Both require preparation and study, yet the spoken word must connect to the hearer in a personal and intimate way. Chrysostom's primary goal was to teach love, but he also tried to encourage integrity and responsibility in his listeners' personal lives.

Chrysostom used the style of dialogue and interplay in his sermons. He created a form wherein he would actually speak the words of each person in the scriptural passage, and then act as moderator to explain their meaning to the congregation. Chrysostom frequently used rhetorical questions in which he presented an ethical or topical challenge to his hearers.[30] For example, in *On the Statues* (Homily 2), he postulated:

Do you wish to be rich?

Have God as a friend . . .

Do you wish to be rich?

Do not be high minded.[31]

Another feature of Chrysostom's preaching was his ability to anticipate objections from his hearers before they had an opportunity to reply.[32] Chrysostom put forth: "Now to prevent your saying, 'How, when liable to such sins, were we justified?'"[33] This technique of preaching, along with metaphors, similes, and word plays, presupposes that the preacher knows his congregation well. These methods of preaching, and many others that he modeled, demonstrated the breadth and freedom that Chrysostom employed in his sermons. He spoke with authority, but this authority was based on the convictions of his faith. This pastoral authority that Chrysostom modeled is the basic difference between spiritual power and secular power; emperors force by command, while a priest attempts to persuade.

A major obstacle that Chrysostom faced in his preaching ministry was that many of his people were ignorant of Scripture and the basic practices of the faith. He attempted to fill that void by offering exegetical sermons on various books of the Bible, weaving into his message practical applications of the faith. An excellent illustration of this teaching skill is found in Chrysostom's sermons on Genesis. Coming on the eve of the Lenten season, he chose this opportunity to instruct the faithful on the benefits of fasting:

> Fasting is nourishment for the soul, you see, and just as bodily nourishment fattens the body, so fasting invigorates the soul, provides it with nimble wings, lifts it on high, enables it to contemplate things that are above, and renders it superior to the pleasures and attractions of this present life. And just as the lightest ships cross the seas more rapidly whereas those weighed down with much cargo take on water, in like manner fasting leaves the faculty of reason nimble and enables it to negotiate the problems of life adroitly and fly to heaven and the things of heaven.[34]

Another example of Chrysostom's exegetical prowess was shown in his detailed parsing of the opening verse of the Gospel of John, "In the beginning was the Word, and the Word was with God":

> The Word is a Being, a distinct Person, proceeding from the Father Himself without alteration. Therefore, just as the expression "In the beginning was the Word" reveals His eternity, so "He was in the beginning with God" has revealed to us His co-eternity. Lest on hearing: "In the beginning was the Word," you might think that He was indeed eternal, but suppose that the life of the Father was older by some interval of time and might consequently concede that the Only-begotten had a beginning, he has added the sentence: "He was in the beginning with God." That is, He was as eternal as the Father Himself, for the Father was never without the Word but always God was with God, though each in His own Person.[35]

Chrysostom had much to say to the clergy, especially as it related to the preaching ministry. He believed that few were naturally gifted homilists but instead gained the ability to preach well through prayer and study.[36] Yet even a well-prepared sermon delivered with expertise may not be met with approval from one's congregation. Chrysostom made clear that pastors should not rely on positive feedback, nor become discouraged when faced with criticism, but instead fulfill their ministry like a loving parent:

> The priest should treat those whom he rules as a father treats very young children. We are not disturbed by children's insults or blows or tears; nor do we think much of their laughter and approval. And so with these people, we should not be much elated by their praise nor much dejected by their censure, when we get these things from them out of season.[37]

In the history of the Church there has rarely been a figure as eminent as John Chrysostom, who excelled as orator, exegete, teacher, witness to and confessor of the Christian faith. His impact and influence has been felt in the Church for sixteen hundred years, inspiring and challenging Christian clergy and lay people with his gift for synthesizing faith and life.

LATER BYZANTINE-ERA PREACHERS

The legacy of prominent preaching did not end with the "Golden Age" of the fourth and fifth centuries. Other voices that followed in Church history also deserve consideration and study. Two specific pillars of the later Byzantine era worthy of attention are John of Damascus and Gregory Palamas. Each faced unique pastoral challenges in his respective era. Furthermore, both preachers in this section broaden the approach to the witness and proclamation of the gospel.

John of Damascus

Though John did not serve in the prototypical position of pastor to a lay flock, his contributions to homiletics and hymnology deserve attention. He was born in Syria in the second half of the seventh century, after the Arabs had conquered it, and when Islam was expanding all around him.

His parents were wealthy, and the family he came from had been Christian for generations. After serving in the civil service, John left to become a monk near Jerusalem. The rest of his biographical information remains limited and sketchy.

Scholars are unclear as to where John preached and to whom he offered his homilies, though these homilies seem to be integrated into the liturgical services of the Church.[38] For contemporary readers it is also difficult to always discern whether the messages being delivered were sermons or written treatises. But what appears certain is that John spoke to a theologically literate audience, one familiar with both Scripture and the writings of Church Fathers.[39]

The dominant controversy during his lifetime was the Iconoclastic Controversy, which took place within the borders of the empire: Emperor Leo III himself decreed that all representations of Christ and the saints be destroyed. In response, John argued that the material flesh of Jesus Christ became a part of his divine person, the visible became visible, and hence it was acceptable to depict Jesus as he is: God became man— God became matter. In his three landmark apologies against those who attacked the divine images (the first two are accepted as sermons), John stated his case unequivocally:

> In former times God, who is without form or body, could never be depicted. But now when God is seen in the flesh conversing with men, I make an image of the God whom I see. I do not worship matter; I worship the Creator of matter who became matter for my sake, who willed to take his abode in matter; who worked out my salvation through matter. Never will I cease honoring the matter which wrought my salvation![40]

John insisted that the Old Testament condemnations of images as idolatry had been misinterpreted. Included in these homilies were extensive selections of patristic passages and historical evidence showing how the use of images had existed in the tradition of the Church for centuries.

A distinguishing feature of John's homilies was his periodic integration of poetic or hymnal material into his messages. In the first of his three preserved sermons on the Dormition of the Theotokos, John wove together theological teachings on the Mother of God not in a dry academic format, but with the tenor of a liturgical hymn:

What shall we say, O Queen? What words shall we use? What praise shall we pour upon thy sacred and glorified head, thou giver of good gifts and of riches, the pride of the human race, the glory of all creation, through whom it is truly blessed. He whom nature did not contain in the beginning, was born of thee. The Invisible One is contemplated face to face. O Word of God, do Thou open my slow lips, and give their utterances Thy richest blessing; inflame us with the grace of Thy Spirit, through whom fishermen became orators, and ignorant men spoke supernatural wisdom, so that our feeble voices may contribute to Thy loved Mother's praises, even though greatness should be extolled by misery. She, the chosen one of an ancient race, by a predetermined counsel and the good pleasure of God the Father, who had begotten Thee in eternity immaterially, brought Thee forth in the latter times, Thou who art propitiation and salvation, justice and redemption, life of life, light of light, and true God of true God.[41]

The other documented homilies delivered by John of Damascus include biblical sermons on the fig tree and the Parable of the Vineyard, a sermon on Holy Saturday, panegyrics on the great martyrs Artemius and Barbara, sermons on the Nativity of the Lord and the Transfiguration of Christ, and the aforementioned sermons on the Dormition of the Theotokos. Although better known for his defense of icons and his work entitled *Fount of Wisdom,* John remains an important voice in the ecclesiastical homiletic dialogue.

Gregory Palamas

Gregory was born in 1296 to an aristocratic family of Asia Minor. He was raised in a pious family, one that enjoyed a close relationship with the Byzantine emperor Andronikos II Paleologos. Gregory became an excellent student in all the academic disciplines of the day, and could have parlayed his relationship with the emperor into a prestigious position within the government. Yet he withdrew from public life and entered the Vatopedi monastery at Mount Athos as a novice. During his monastic experience, Gregory was introduced to the practice of "prayer of the heart," a means of mental prayer and solitude that is often termed *hesychasm.*

Gregory eventually served as pastor to communities in Thessaloniki, modeling the spiritual practices of the early Desert Fathers. In the 1330s events took place in the life of the Church that placed Gregory among the most significant apologists of Orthodoxy and brought him great renown as a teacher and preacher. The principle controversy of his day involved the fundamental distinction between the essence and energies of God. The learned monk Barlaam, a trained academician, challenged the practice of the hesychasts, stating that it was impossible to know the essence of God. Barlaam labeled prayer of the heart as heretical, thus challenging Gregory to defend his position. Gregory explained that in prayer, man is filled from within with the eternal glory, with the divine light experienced at the Transfiguration of Christ on Mount Tabor. This truth is elaborated upon in the *Life* of the saint:

> For that prayer [the Jesus Prayer] is true and perfect which fills the soul with Divine grace and spiritual gifts. As chrism perfumes the jar the more strongly the tighter it is closed, so prayer, the more fast it is imprisoned in the heart, abounds the more in Divine grace . . . By [this prayer] the dew of the Holy Spirit is brought down upon the heart, as Elijah brought down rain on Mount Carmel. This mental prayer reaches to the very throne of God and is preserved in golden vials . . . This mental prayer is the light which illumines man's soul and inflames his heart with the fire of love of God. It is the chain linking God with man and man with God.[42]

While serving in the role as archbishop of Thessalonika, Gregory's homilies offered a consistent balance between originality of thought and strict adherence to the tradition of his predecessors. Although capable of dispensing deep theoretical axioms, Gregory instead conveyed refreshingly practical explanations of the faith. He often used the liturgical cycle of services and the rhythm of the Church calendar as opportunities to feed his flock. In a sermon offered on the Annunciation of the Theotokos, Gregory beautifully expounds on the person of Mary:

> Surely it is obvious to anyone that the Virgin Mary is both the burning bush and the tongs. She conceived the divine fire within her and was not burnt, and through her the Bearer of the sins of the world was united with the human race, purifying us thoroughly by means of this indescribable bond. The Virgin Mother, and she alone, is the frontier between created and uncreated nature. All who know God will recognize her as the one who contained Him Who cannot be contained. All who sing hymns

to God will praise her next after Him . . . She is the theme of the
prophets, the first of the Apostles, the support of the martyrs,
the dais of the teachers. She is the glory of those on earth, the de-
light of those in heaven, the adornment of the whole Creation.
She is the beginning, fount and root of the hope stored up for
us in heaven.[43]

The contributions of Gregory came at a crucial time in the history
of the Church, when Christian thought was threatened by both outside
forces (Islamic threats to the region), and internal queries (Barlaam and
his disciple Akyndinos). He did not provide an exhaustive system capable
of answering all problems, but conferred to his flock the stability and
wisdom of the Church—a skill that homilists should take note of.

The Preaching Ministry
of Kosmas Aitolos

During the Ottoman occupation of the Balkans between the fifteenth
and nineteenth centuries, the Orthodox Church was unable to freely live
out its beliefs and practices. From this restrictive environment rose an
eminent preacher named Kosmas, born in 1714 in the western region of
Greece called Aitolia. Though initially drawn to the monastic life, Kosmas experienced a calling to preach and received permission from Patriarch Sophronios to become an itinerant preacher. For the next nineteen
years, Kosmas traveled on foot, by donkey, and by ship to the poorest
villages in what is today the lands of Greece, Turkey, and Albania.

Kosmas used the homiletic approach that Jesus implemented, taking
illustrations from the experiences and surroundings with which his audiences were familiar. The content of his sermons was simple, encouraging,
and gentle. His humility and ability to identify with the struggles of the
people made his homilies endearing and effective. Here is one example
of that preaching style:

If it were possible for me to climb up into the sky, to be able to
shout with a great voice, to preach to the entire world that only
our Christ is the Son and Word of God, true God and the life
of all, I would have done it. But because I can't do such a big
thing, I do this small thing: I walk from place to place and teach

my brethren as I can, not as a teacher but as a brother. Only our Christ is a teacher.[44]

Within his preaching ministry, Kosmas addressed the social injustices and abuses of his time, and this eventually led to his martyrdom. Village elders, landowners, and wealthy merchants felt their interests threatened when Kosmas called for just taxation, fair prices, and equitable rents:[45]

You elders who are heads of the villages, if you wish to be saved, should love all the Christians as your children and should apportion taxes according to each person's ability to pay and not play favorites.[46]

Education was the backbone of Kosmas's messages. Rather than simply theorize about the importance of literacy, Kosmas was responsible for the construction of schools and reading resources. The most comprehensive and descriptive summary on the life of Kosmas Aitolos is offered by the author and compiler of his biography:

His love, concern, and tireless labor among ordinary people, his honest and forthright preaching, his unassuming character, his sterling and uncompromising personality, and his great love for and dedication to Jesus Christ earned for him the titles of "Equal to the Apostles," "Teacher of the Greek Nation," and the "Apostle of the Poor."[47]

THE COLLECTIVE TEACHINGS OF THE GREAT HOMILISTS

What are the valuable nuggets of wisdom that can be gleaned from this august group of homilists? The possibilities are infinite. For the sake of brevity, let us consider several points that might be beneficial for contemporary preachers.

First and foremost, the homilists all insist that a good preacher know Scripture and tradition, and live them in his daily life. A proficient preacher must have a working knowledge of the dogmatic, canonical, sacramental, and liturgical practices of the faith. He continually strives to study and prepare an edifying message and does not simply rely on past successes.

A preacher will be ineffective and subject to valid criticism if the message offered is incongruent with the homilist's own life. Because he is their shepherd and guide, the congregation will demand accountability and consistency in their pastor's life. Furthermore, the preacher must accept that he is simply the communicator of the gospel—a vehicle of the Holy Spirit. The focus of his preaching ministry must always be on Christ, not on himself.

A second lesson conveyed to contemporary preachers from our wise elders is that a holistic approach to pastoral ministry requires us to see preaching as only one part of our ministry, albeit an integral one. In the Orthodox tradition, preaching is not an independent spiritual gift, but one of many avenues for shepherding the flock. Joseph Allen comments:

> One's sermons are to facilitate, to prepare the soil of the soul, to cause the heart to be receptive and responsive to the gospel . . . "What" is preached interacts with all that is attempted in the pastor's ministry.[48]

Allen emphasizes that preaching is simply communicating ideas, yet the words of a sermon have the power to build a sense of communion within a congregation—a necessary aspiration of the pastor.

A third way in which we see the greatness of the preachers we have spoken about is their treatment of the issue of pluralism in their preaching. Many people erroneously believe that pluralism is a contemporary homiletic concern. However, a careful reading of historical sermons reveals that preachers have always needed to address the issues of their day, whether those issues were secularism, materialism, false Christian teachings, or alternative lifestyles and ideologies. Preachers must inform and teach the fundamentals of the gospel so that their flock can articulate the faith within a pluralistic society. Topical sermons are imperative so that the members of the congregation can connect the faith with their daily challenges.

A fourth approach to preaching used by our forebears can be found in their use of the liturgical calendar to its full advantage. Preachers can weave dogmatic, scriptural, and ethical lessons within their sermons, allowing the liturgical rhythm of the Church to formulate their message. Again, Joseph Allen offers a helpful observation:

> Some examples are the following: *Advent*: waiting, expectation, promise; *Christmas*: Christ's birth and incarnation in our lives,

stirrings, growing spiritually; *Epiphany*: how God reveals himself to us, light, manifestation, its connection with the Nativity; *Triodion* and *Great Lent*: Christ's sacrifice and the place of sacrificial love and repentance in our lives; *Easter*: Resurrection and death in our own lives, hope, forgiveness; *Pentecost*: life, spirit, renewal, recreation; *Trinity*: community of faith, community of persons, etc.; *Hagiography*: Saint's lives and our own, etc.[49]

A fifth observation to be culled from the lineage of Church history is the varied approach of the great preachers to delivery and execution. Every communicator has a unique style—a certain way of developing ideas, forming sentences, crafting language, and using words. The preaching giants of the past did not mimic other great homilists. They developed their own styles based on the gifts that God blessed them with. Each preacher brings a unique history, personality, and perspective into the pulpit. As we attempt various techniques, we learn our strengths and weaknesses, and we can adapt accordingly. The collective corpus of the great Church homilists reassures the contemporary preacher of the truth of this advice: trust that, together with your sincere effort, the Holy Spirit will inspire, invigorate, and propel your preaching for the glory of God.

PART II

SELECTED SERMONS

Sermons for Fall

Isolation and Community Life

There was a study completed recently on the medical effects of loneliness and, by contrast, the benefits of community life. This study focused on a small band of Italians who left Roseto Valfortore, a small village in Italy, and arrived in America about a hundred years ago in hopes of a better life. Settling in eastern Pennsylvania, the immigrants named their village Roseto. There the members of this group re-created the strong community ties they had nurtured in Italy. They lived in three-generation households, centered their lives on family, and built their houses so close together that all it took to have a neighborly chat was to walk to the front porch.

By the 1960s, Roseto had become a magnet for researchers. It seems that although the residents of Roseto shared the same water supply, doctors, and hospitals with nearby villages, they had only 40% as many heart attacks. At first researchers thought the Rosetans might carry some special, protective genes. But this was not the case, for Rosetans who moved away, even to nearby towns, lost whatever magic the community possessed against heart disease. That magic, now known as the "Roseto Effect," is as simple as it is elusive in America today: close ties with other people.

The medical study concluded that closeness with other people has a strong protective effect against illness and death. Conversely, the lack of such ties—social isolation—can kill just as surely as smoking, obesity, or high blood pressure. Implied in this study is the conclusion that loneliness is not simply a painful experience, but a major public health problem.

Certainly the ability to spend time alone happily—creative solitude, if you will—is one of the great joys of life and a hallmark of a mature person. But scientific evidence supports the assertion that social isolation—that is, having few meaningful personal ties—can have severe medical consequences. Conversely, close ties with people can significantly increase health and longevity.

What would the Christian response be to this fascinating research? Effectively, this data affirms what is already self-evident about the nature of Christianity: the Church is not composed of isolated individuals, each searching for their salvation apart from one another and apart from God. Rather, the Church is a communal organism, described in the New Testament as "the body of Christ." Each member of the body performs an important function, with no one part more valuable than another. This interdependent body represents a systemic union, with Christ as the head of the body.

Even the Trinity is a community of persons: Father, Son, and Spirit. They are three separate persons, yet even the Trinity sees everything in the context of relationships. Just as the Trinity lives in community with each other and with us, so man and woman—being made in God's image—become fully human by living a life of sharing and reciprocity.

The early Church illustrated this reality in very practical ways. The apostles recognized the need to use all the members of the fledgling Church to serve one another based on the gifts that each member possessed. The faithful in the book of Acts looked after each other, using personal resources for the care of the body of believers. In 1 Corinthians 12, Paul wrote that "we are members one of another," so that any action performed by any member of a church community inevitably affected all the other members. The same reality holds true today, just as it did in the early days of the Church.

Many Americans, young and old, turn to therapists, self-help groups, and medications to combat isolation. But the body of Christ, the Church, offers holy and relevant alternatives. Through communal worship, the sacraments, fellowship, study groups, service to others, and witness, the Church meets the social needs inherent in all of us. It is the personal relationships and emotional interdependency found in Christian communities that fill people's needs for, and deepen, long-term intimacy.

The grace of the Lord Jesus Christ and the love of God and the fellowship of the Holy Spirit be with you all. (2 Cor 13:14)

CONTEMPORARY ATHEISM

Christopher Hitchens is a British-American author and journalist. His controversial style is fully evident in his recent book, entitled *God is Not Great: How Religion Poisons Everything*. Hitchens, among others, has developed a recent genre that has gained in popularity in bookstores and blogs: atheistic literature. I recently read Hitchens's book, and he boils down his attack on religion to four points. Allow me to highlight his four points and then address each one from a Christian perspective.

1. "Religious faith . . . misrepresents the origins of man and the cosmos."

2. Because of this misrepresentation, religion maximizes a state of servility.

3. Religion is "the cause of dangerous sexual repression."

4. Religion "is ultimately grounded on wish-thinking."[1]

Let's address these points one by one. The author's first claim is that religion "misrepresents the origins of man and the cosmos." The statement implies that faith rejects science—that one must choose between faith and science. From a Christian perspective, nothing could be further from the truth. The Church has always expressed appreciation for the sciences and views science as a gift from God. Many of the saints of the Church were physicians, astronomers, and students of various disciplines in the scientific community.

What is the Church's teaching on the origins of man and the cosmos? Simply that God is the Creator of all things and that the human person is made in the image of God. Being "in the image" does not imply that we physically look like God, but rather that we can aspire to develop traits and virtues that mirror God. The Church does not reject the existence of dinosaurs or even the many theories of evolution; it simply demands that the presence of God be accepted somewhere in the creative process.

Hitchens's second criticism is that religion maximizes a state of servility. Practicing Christians accept this criticism with open arms. We see ourselves as glad and willing servants of God, and we view God as a loving and caring father whose benevolence is illustrated beautifully in the Parable of the Prodigal Son. Hitchens, however, likens servility to slavery. Conversely, Christianity views being a servant of God as a loving response to a Deity who loves us so much that his Son was incarnated to live and die for us.

The author's third assessment is that religion dangerously suppresses sexuality. A careful reading of Scripture and the Orthodox marriage service illustrates that sexual relations within marriage are a gift of joy. The Church does not teach that sexual relations are only for the purposes of procreation. Rather, it sees sexuality as a loving expression between the married couple. For our own protection, however, the Church treasures sexuality within marriage only, guarding us from the spiritual scarring of broken relationships, the tragedy of children who are cast aside, sexually transmitted diseases, and other consequences of the abuse of this divine gift.

The final criticism leveled by the author is that religion is ultimately grounded on wishful thinking. Here Hitchens is focusing on blind faith, which the Church rejects. The basis of the Christian faith is a living relationship with Jesus Christ. Christians should not believe in God because the Bible tells them to or because their pious grandmother demands that they do so; the Christian faith must be accepted as a free gift and experienced in the deepest recesses of their being. Like any healthy relationship, a Christian's connection with God must include dialogue, sacrifice, perseverance, and mutual understanding. A blind faith is a weak faith.

While it is true that religious people have not always lived out their faith appropriately, and in some cases have even lived disastrously, Hitchens is naïve to dismiss or reject religion categorically. Briefly consider Jesus's (and the Christian Church's) influence on civil laws, the democratic process, humanitarian institutions such as hospitals, orphanages, schools, and food shelters, not to mention on art, music, and literature.

You may think that I would discourage you from reading Hitchens's book and other materials on atheism—but the opposite is true. To be fully informed about the Christian faith implies being open to dialogue, even to provocative and critical writings. Reading such materials can even strengthen or better inform our faith. Be encouraged and comforted by the words of Christ: "In the world you face persecution. But take courage; I have conquered the world!" (John 16:33).

STEWARDSHIP SUNDAY

Today, on Stewardship Sunday, each member of our community is invited to make a financial commitment for the
ministry of our parish. The topic of stewardship makes some people uncomfortable. Some believe that money issues should not be discussed in
church, the argument being that our focus should on spiritual issues such
as prayer, good works, and the kingdom of heaven.

Yet a closer look at Scripture reveals many interesting facts about
finances. For example, there are approximately five hundred verses in the
Bible that relate to prayer, but over twenty-three hundred verses that refer
to wealth, possessions, and stewardship. Amazingly, one out of every six
verses in the Gospel books of Matthew, Mark, Luke, and John alludes to
financial issues. One out of six verses! Since stewardship was important
enough for Jesus to teach his followers on a regular basis, we also should
become better acquainted with this topic.

Let's start with a working definition. The word *oikonomos*, often ren-
dered "stewardship" in translations of the New Testament, is a compound
word consisting of two Greek words: one translated as "house," and the
other as "administrator" or "manager." A steward, therefore, is one who
manages a household. For Christians, stewardship is the wise manage-
ment of God's resources.

Many of Jesus's parables emphasize the stewardship of time, talent,
and finances. He speaks of the prodigal son, who spends his money care-
lessly, and of the Pharisee, who is improperly preoccupied with his possessions. Though his message is spiritual, Jesus frequently comments on
the material, noting that there is a relationship between the two, para-
doxical though it seems.

At this point in my presentation, I am sure that I have not convinced
anyone to increase his or her stewardship commitment for next year. And
do you know why? First, definitions of stewardship will not change one's
heart. Second, Scripture verses on the topic of stewardship will probably
not motivate anyone, either. Thus my personal plea for increased stewardship will likely fall on deaf ears.

Instead, I believe that the most effective method of increasing stewardship is to be inspired by a role model, an example. When we witness

others who are good stewards of their time, talent, and possessions, we will make stewardship a way of life.

One of my own role models for stewardship is my grandmother. A few examples from her life shaped my commitment to stewardship.

First, the stewardship of time. I would often stay at my grandmother's house for weeks at a time during summer vacation. She would take me to church services on Sunday. On weekdays, my grandmother would rise early, offer her daily prayers, and cense the house. Because I slept in the room where the icon corner was located, she would unintentionally wake me from a deep sleep while censing the house. One day I asked her why she was praying, since it was not Sunday. She responded lovingly, "God blesses us seven days a week. Should we not do the same?" I learned at that moment about the stewardship of time. God gives each of us the gift of twenty-four hours. Certainly we can find a portion of that time to share with God our praise, our problems, our thanks, and our love.

Second, the stewardship of talent. My grandmother was very active in the life of the Church: she participated in the choir, Philoptochos, festivals, etc. But the occasions when she took me to the hospital to visit people made the greatest impression on me. Being a patient can be lonely, frightening, and painful, so receiving a visit is usually appreciated and comforting. First my grandmother would take me to rooms of people she knew. Then she would take the extra step: after visiting the people she knew, she would peek into other hospital rooms to see if someone else might benefit from a warm conversation. This spoke volumes about the stewardship of talent. In her hospital visits, my grandmother used her gifts of compassion, conversation, and concern for others. Stewardship of talent is applying the gifts that God has given us to serve our parish and the community at large.

Third, the stewardship of possessions. My grandparents raised their three children during the Depression years of the 1930s, when many people suffered terrible financial hardships. The neighborhood where my grandparents lived also housed people who struggled to support their families. It was a common practice for my grandmother to prepare a plate of food and bring it to a neighbor in need—not the leftovers, but the first fruits. During my childhood, my grandmother continued this practice by preparing a covered dish and delivering it to someone in need.

I share these reflections not for sentimental reasons, but to highlight how one person, one witness, made a permanent impression on me about the power of stewardship. Stewardship must be modeled by people we love and trust. Once we see that example in others, we will be inspired to follow suit.

Before the stewardship cards are distributed and filled out, I want to leave you with one last thought. And that is: What motivates us to give? If the feeling is "you must," then you will give out of coercion and without freedom. If the feeling is "you ought to," then you will be a steward out of moral obligation and a feeling of duty. Instead, my hope is that we will return our stewardship commitment cards with a feeling of "I *want* to." If so, we will be motivated by grace, freedom, and love for God and others.

THE PARABLES OF JESUS

I have yet to meet a person who does not like a good story. Stories inspire a spirit of wonder and adventure. We learn at an early age that stories can transmit messages with deep wisdom. Even as adults, we are mesmerized by a good storyteller, who paints words and images on the canvas of our imagination.

One of history's most capable storytellers was a young, itinerant Galilean named Jesus, whose stories are known as parables. The word *parable* comes from the Greek meaning "to place alongside," because parables use the familiar to explain the unfamiliar. Simply put, a parable is a story with religious meaning drawn from ordinary life. It's easy to keep the meaning of the biblical parables at arm's length by limiting their relevance to the time and place of Jesus. But people who read the Gospels seriously know that when reading a parable one always asks, "What is its meaning—for then, for now, for all time?"

Certainly, all of the parables are historically and culturally conditioned. When Jesus originally told them, they had meaning for his immediate audience. Sometimes Jesus shocked his immediate audience, as when he presented God through a compassionate Samaritan. Less startling would have been the parables Jesus told of the Sower and the Seed, or the Parable of the Talents. All of the parables contained images and metaphors that Jesus's original audience would have immediately understood.

Limiting the meaning of Jesus's parables to their original time and culture, however, would do them a great disservice. The parables of Jesus continue to have meaning today. Contemporary Christians, like those in the past, want to know how persistent they should be in prayer. Reading or hearing the Parable of the Persistent Widow helps them maintain their vigilance. Others want to know if God hears our prayers. Encountering the Parable of the Friend at Midnight gives them a response. People of faith today want to know what they need to do to enjoy ultimate union with God. The Parable of the Last Judgment gives them food for thought. Many twenty-first-century Christians wonder if God forgives us for the mistakes we make. The forgiveness of the father in the Parable of the Prodigal Son clearly addresses this concern.

Parables have meaning for today because they continue to address the issues and situations that we all encounter on the pilgrimage of life. Parables inspire us to ponder anew who we are and what is required of us by God.

Parables are open-ended stories. It is up to the hearer or the reader to complete their meaning. In the book of Mark, chapter 4, Jesus states, "Let anyone with ears to hear listen" (v. 9). Jesus implies that there is a response that is demanded of the listener. Parables raise deep and important questions: Where is our treasure? What kind of ground do we provide for the seed of God? What does it mean to be compassionate? How do poverty and wealth impinge upon the practice of justice and faith? Parables do not simply recount a clever tale. Rather, they challenge a person's conscience, causing reflection and at times discomfort, but always calling one to action.

I am sure that everyone has a favorite parable, a teaching of Jesus that has moved him or her. But regardless of which ones are our favorites, the reality is that all of the parables of Jesus continue to intrigue, inspire, puzzle, challenge, and amuse all who encounter them.

BALANCING FAITH AND FEAR

Why does God seem so far away?
When will God do something for me?
When will the evil people of this world get what they deserve?

Very similar questions are posed by Habakkuk, the Old Testament prophet, whom we honor on December 2. We don't know that much about the man—other than that his name is difficult to pronounce! We do know that he was a contemporary of Jeremiah and that he ministered in the time right before the Babylonians destroyed the northern kingdom of the Jews, several hundred years before Christ.

Habakkuk had a number of questions and complaints for God. This short book is actually a dialogue between the prophet and God, with Habakkuk arguing that God's ways are sometimes unfathomable and even unjust. So what can contemporary Christians learn from this ancient and obscure book?

First, I believe that we can acquire knowledge about prayer when we follow the direct and honest approach used by Habakkuk. In the opening verses of chapter 1, the prophet writes, "O Lord, how long shall I cry for help, and you will not listen? Or cry to you 'violence' and you will not save? . . . Why do you look on the treacherous, and are silent when the wicked swallow those more righteous than they?" (Hab 1:2, 13). Habakkuk asks a question of God and describes his complaint. From this we learn that suffering and adversity can often be an important starting point in prayer. By expressing sorrow, pain, and grief to God, we begin the healing process with openness and expectation.

A second facet of this book, experienced by Habakkuk and shared by every devout Christian, is fear. Habakkuk demonstrates to us that true faith often includes an element of fear. He teaches us how to move from the trenches of real-life struggles to a mature and true faith in God. I mentioned earlier that at the time this book was written the Jews were about to be invaded by the Babylonians. Listen to what Habakkuk wrote in verse 3:16: "I heard and my heart pounded, my lips quivered at the sound; decay crept into my bones, and my legs trembled" (NIV). Habakkuk trusted God and lived a holy life, yet he was very afraid of the

Babylonian invasion God had told him was coming. Note the many ana-
tomical terms he uses to describe his fear. He says his heart pounded, his
lips quivered, and his legs trembled. He used these terms to show that
he was shaking with fear throughout his whole being. Surely a person of
true faith doesn't have fear like that—or does he? This mighty prophet of
God, this great man of faith, trembled like a leaf in the face of his threat-
ening circumstances.

Habakkuk isn't alone, either. We find in the pages of Scripture that
Abraham was fearful when faced with uncertainty, that King David admitted that his courage was failing him in spite of his faith, and that the
prophet Jeremiah felt he could not face the obstacles before him.

Even the illustrious apostle Paul offers a telling glimpse into his inner
life in 2 Corinthians when he writes, "For when we came into Macedo-
nia, our bodies had no rest, but we were afflicted in every way—disputes
without and fears within" (7:5). Imagine *Paul* expressing fear!

The overriding message of Habakkuk is that we can be faithful and
committed to God and still experience moments of fear. In times of trouble we are encouraged to share our fears with God and others, seeking the
peace and reassurance that can come only from God. We live in fearful
times, not knowing what the future holds. We are vulnerable to terror-
ism, unexpected illness, unemployment, or a senseless shooting. Faith
and fear sometimes walk hand in hand.

But the author of this book does not leave us with only our fears.
He concludes by writing the powerful and eloquent verses found in
chapter 3:

> Though the fig tree does not blossom, and no fruit is on the
> vines; though the produce of the olive fails and the fields yield
> no food; though the flock is cut off from the fold and there is
> no herd in the stalls, yet I will rejoice in the Lord; I will exult
> in the God of my salvation. God, the Lord, is my strength.
> (vv. 17–18)

Habakkuk looks back and recalls the times in his life when God sup-
ported and guided him. Even when his foundation is shaking all
around him, Habakkuk trusts in the Lord for strength and hope in the
future. May we also find comfort in the life and example of Habakkuk
the prophet.

A SONG OF PRAISE

D o the words *Parakletike, Triodion, Pentecostarion,* and
Menaion mean anything to you? Probably not, unless you
are a devout lover of Orthodox Church music. These words are titles of
books of hymns that make up part of the vast collection of Byzantine music. Hymns that have been collected from the third century up to the present day and are used in our worship are found in these precious volumes.

Hymns are sacred poetry that are set to music and sung as part of the
worship services of the Church. In the early days of the Church, hymns
from the Hebrew tradition were used—predominantly the Psalms. Soon
after, distinctly Christian compositions were introduced.

Generally speaking, two types of hymns developed in the course
of Orthodox hymnology: those intended to awaken the emotion of the
worshipper, and those designed to teach a theological truth. For example,
a hymn intended to evoke a worshipper's emotions could be as follows:

Seeing you crucified, O Christ, all creation trembled;
the foundations of the earth shook from fear of your power.
For today by being raised up,
the veil of the temple was torn in two,
the tombs were opened, and the dead rose from the graves.
The centurion shuddered when he saw the miracle;
your mother stood near, and cried with a mother's lamentation:
"How can I not mourn and be overwhelmed when I see you
nailed, hanging as a criminal on the tree?"
O Lord, you were crucified and buried and rose from the dead,
glory to you. (Hymn from Matins on Holy Friday)

An example of a more theological, or dogmatic, hymn is as follows:

Before the ages the Father begat me,
who am Wisdom and Creator,
and he established me as the beginning of his ways.
He appointed me to perform the works
which now are mystically accomplished.
For though I am by nature the uncreated Word,
I make my own the speech and qualities of the humanity
that I have assumed. (Hymn from Matins on Holy Thursday)

These are only two examples of the multitude of hymns that are part of the liturgical music tradition of the Orthodox Church. For instance, the *Parakletike* contains hymns for the eight-week cycle of the Matins and Vespers services. The *Triodion* serves as the liturgical book for Lent, the ten weeks before Pascha. After the *Triodion* comes a special book for the services of Holy and Great Week, and then the *Pentecostarion* follows. Covering fifty days (hence its name), the *Pentecostarion* begins with Pascha, includes the week of Pentecost, and ends on the Sunday of All Saints. The *Menaia* are the collections of hymns celebrating the saints throughout the year, one book for each month.

Although we primarily know these hymns in the context of communal worship, singing or listening to music can be a holy and healthy expression of our personal prayer time as well. The opportunities and resources available to learn and immerse ourselves in the Orthodox musical tradition are numerous:

- Speak to one of our chanters or our choir director, who will show you the many Church hymnals that are used in liturgical worship throughout the year.

- Sing hymns from any period of the Church year during your personal prayer time, including: Christ is Risen (Paschal troparion, or hymn), Lord of the Powers (Lenten hymn), the hymn of our parish, the hymn (or apolytikion) of your saint, selections from the Paraklesis to the Theotokos (usually chanted the first two weeks of August), etc.

- Order a compact disc from an Orthodox resource center or bookstore and listen to selections during your prayer time or in the car.

Make a joyful noise to God, all the earth;
sing the glory of his name; give to him glorious praise.
(Ps 66:1–2)

THE BEAUTY OF CREATION

Autumn is a lovely time of year. The leaves are changing. The end of the harvest season has produced fresh fruits and vegetables for our sustenance. The warm and lazy summer season is behind us, and the raw and dormant winter lies ahead.

Everyone can appreciate the various expressions of nature: hiking in the mountains, a walk along the shoreline, a visit to a botanical garden. Nature has a way of calming our souls; we are awed by the complexities and detail of creation. It revitalizes and restores our whole being.

Yet there are two contrasting extremes being played out in the world today, two radical paths evolving concurrently. One is the exploitation of creation and nature, and the other is the worship of creation and nature.

Let's first explore the exploitation of nature. Without suggesting political or corporate biases, the reality is that the capitalistic systems of the world pursue progress and profit at the expense of ecological concerns. Worldwide acid rain, climate change, global warming, air and water pollution, toxic waste, the destruction of the rain forest, and the accelerating loss of species are all directly related to economic, political, and capitalistic frameworks. The threat of ecological catastrophe looms large as the pace of our industrial progress quickens.

At the other end of the spectrum, we find a renewal of earth religions, those which worship creation and nature. Walk into any local bookstore and you will find entire sections devoted to modern paganism, Wicca, and other religions that view nature itself as a deity. These earth-based religions are not new; they have existed for thousands of years. This renewal could perhaps be a response to how nature is being devalued and exploited.

But what is the Orthodox perspective on these two extremes? The easiest place to begin is by reviewing the Nicene Creed, which is recited at each Divine Liturgy. The very first verse states, "I believe in one God, the Father Almighty, Creator of heaven and earth . . ." Our faith teaches that nature was created by the will of God. Creation is therefore a free act, a gratuitous act of God. Creator and creation are distinct. We worship God, not creation.

Following the creation of things visible and invisible, God gave humankind specific instructions on how to relate to nature. In the book of Genesis, God gives us dominion over the earth, to preserve and cultivate creation (1:28). The most appropriate term used to describe our relationship with nature is *stewardship*. In Psalm 24 we read, "The earth is the Lord's and all that is in it, the world, and those who live in it" (v. 1). From these verses we see that God is the Creator of nature, and we as humans are called to nurture and care for his creation. According to God's original instructions, humankind's stewardship responsibilities are to cultivate, protect, and rightfully use this gift of creation.

It may be helpful to offer several modern examples of good stewardship, examples of harmonious relationships with nature found in various cultures. The Native American Indians are cited frequently as good stewards because of their incredible attunement to the natural world. Their hunting practices, for example, allowed them to derive their sustenance from the earth for thousands of years without in any way destroying the animal and plant species that they use for food. Similarly, the Amish have—in their quiet way—developed a life that is agriculturally based, living close to the soil and remaining utterly dedicated to the sacredness of nature and its relationship with the Divine.

Our own Patriarch Bartholomew has been labeled the "Green Patriarch" for organizing several international conferences on protecting the environment. The patriarch reminds us that all creation has the capacity to sanctify, and to bring glory to God. In a recent article published in the *Wall Street Journal*, the patriarch stated:

> Climate change, pollution and the exploitation of our natural resources are commonly seen as the domain not of priests but rather of politicians, scientists, technocrats or interest groups organized by concerned citizens. What does preserving the planet have to do with saving the soul? A lot, as it turns out. For if life is sacred, so is the entire web that sustains it . . . Is this an issue for Caesar or for God? We believe it must be approached in both its political and spiritual dimensions. Climate change will only be overcome when all of us—scientists and politicians, theologians and economists, specialists and lay citizens—cooperate for the common good.[2]

When contemplating conservation as an ethical act, we should bear in mind a poetic and metaphorical speech delivered in 1854 by a Native

American Indian named Chief Seattle. His eloquent thoughts capture the essence of ecological stewardship:

> The Great Chief in Washington [the President of the United States] sends words that he wishes to buy our land . . . How can you buy or sell the sky, the warmth of the land? The idea is strange to us. If we do not own the freshness of the air and the sparkle of the water, how can you buy them?
>
> Every part of this earth is sacred to my people. Every shining pine needle, every sandy shore, every mist in the dark woods, every humming insect is holy in the memory and experience of my people. Teach your children what we have taught our children; respect the earth. Whatever befalls the earth befalls the children of the earth, this we know. The earth does not belong to man; man belongs to earth. All things are connected. Man did not weave the web of life; he is merely a strand in it. Whatever he does to the web, he does to himself.[3]

As we enjoy the next few weeks of fall foliage, let us always remain in awe of God's wonderful creation.

ST. DEMETRIUS

A few weeks before Christmas in 1917, the beautiful, snowy landscapes of Europe were blackened by war. It was World War I; the trenches on one side held the Germans, and the other side Americans. Separating them was a very narrow strip of no-man's-land. A young German soldier attempting to cross that no-man's-land was shot and became entangled in the barbed wire. He cried out in anguish.

Between the shells, all the Americans in that sector heard him scream. When one American soldier could stand it no longer, he left the American trenches and, on his stomach, crawled out to that German soldier. When the Americans realized what he was doing, they stopped firing. Then a German officer realized what the young American was doing and also ordered his men to cease fire.

Now there was an eerie silence in the air. Still on his stomach, the American made his way to the German soldier and disentangled him. He stood up with the German in his arms, walked straight to the German trenches, and placed him in the waiting arms of his comrades. Having done so, he turned and started back to the American trenches.

Suddenly there was a hand on his shoulder that spun him around. There stood a German officer who had won the Iron Cross, the highest German honor for bravery. He jerked it from his own uniform and placed it on the American, who walked back to the American trenches. When he was safely in the trenches, they resumed the insanity of war![4]

I share this story with you because the themes that are highlighted are warfare, soldiers, courage, and compassion. These same four characteristics were imbued in St. Demetrius, whose memory we honor today.

St. Demetrius was born and educated in Thessalonica in the third century. His father was a military commander, and when he died the emperor appointed Demetrius in his place as military commander of Thessalonica. Soon after Demetrius's appointment, the emperor ordered him to persecute the Christians in that region. Demetrius not only disobeyed the emperor, he openly confessed Christ to the entire city.

The emperor was furious. He summoned Demetrius and demanded that he renounce Christ; Demetrius refused. The enraged emperor cast him into prison and sent soldiers to torture and kill him. After Demetrius's execution, Christians recovered his body and buried it, and from it flowed healing myrrh, by which many of the sick were cured.

We could easily treat St. Demetrius's biography as though it were just another record of a historical figure who gave his life for Christ. However, the witness of St. Demetrius offers us important lessons that we can apply in many aspects of our lives, but particularly in the area of spiritual warfare—being a soldier for Christ.

This kind of military language might seem contrary to the message of Christ and to the Christian life. But Jesus teaches his followers that we must enter heaven by force. This means that we cannot grow in Christ as passive observers; instead, we must actively pursue the kingdom of heaven.

Demetrius's life as a soldier in the Roman Empire helps us understand the Church's practice of anointing the whole body of someone just before he or she is baptized. This practice is performed to recall a similar tradition that took place in the Roman Empire: before a soldier entered the battlefield, oil was spread over his body. This reduced infections as well as provided other medicinal benefits.

The Church continues this practice by spreading oil on the catechumen just before baptism to help us remember that the person being baptized will immediately enter the spiritual battlefield. The newly illumined will become a soldier for Christ. He or she, and all members of the Church, will continue to battle Satan and all evil influences from the day of our baptism until our last breath.

St. Paul, in his Letter to the Ephesians, also uses military imagery in describing the spiritual life:

> Be strong in the Lord and in the strength of his power. Put on the whole armor of God, so that you may be able to stand against the wiles of the devil . . . Fasten the belt of truth around your waist, and put on the breastplate of righteousness . . . Take the shield of faith, with which you will be able to quench all the flaming arrows of the evil one. Take the helmet of salvation, and the sword of the Spirit, which is the word of God. (Eph 6:10–11, 14, 16–17)

As difficult as the fight may be, the Church has given us the tools— or if you will, the weapons—necessary to be victorious in this spiritual warfare: prayer, Scripture, the liturgical cycle of services, the sacraments, fasting, and more. When we arm ourselves with these precious spiritual weapons, we are assured of victory in this unseen warfare. The life of St. Demetrius inspires us to fight the good fight and to take the kingdom of heaven by storm.

> O victorious Demetrius, you were given to the world
> as a powerful protector against dangers,
> and an invincible soldier of Christ.
> As you inspired Nestor to overcome the pride of Lyaios,
> so intercede with Christ God that he may grant us his great
> mercy. (Troparion of St. Demetrius)

BREAD OF LIFE (THANKSGIVING)

The wonder of the Thanksgiving feast in America is that the holiday transcends all ethnic, cultural, and religious boundaries. The family dinner table is garnished with every imaginable delicacy, influenced by one's background and imagination. Besides the traditional turkey, bread is the one food item that is found at most every Thanksgiving table. Bread is as universal as it is varied. Just a sampling of breads that are found around the world includes:

- America – sliced bread
- France – croissant, baguette
- Italian – Italian bread, focaccia
- Jewish/Eastern Europe – bagel
- Mexico – tortilla
- Greece – tsoureki
- India – nan
- Middle East – pita
- Germany – pumpernickel
- Kenya – chipotti
- England – muffin
- Israel – challah

The wide use of bread in the world is not a phenomenon limited to the present age. In biblical times bread played a major *roll* (pun intended!) in people's lives. A large portion of everyday life revolved around the production, distribution, preparation, and consumption of bread (and wheat). Bread crossed over every boundary of biblical times—social, political, economic, cultural, and institutional. Bread was truly universally understood. Perhaps that is why God utilized bread to convey universal truths in the Scriptures: the Hebrew word for bread (*lehem*) is used almost three hundred times in the Old Testament, and in the New Testament the Greek word for bread (*artos*) is mentioned almost one hundred times.

In the Old Testament, we are first introduced to bread during the oppression of the Israelites by the Egyptians. Through their covenant with Abraham, the Hebrews were God's chosen people. Unfortunately, they later came under the domination of the Egyptian pharaoh. The Lord spoke to Moses and instructed the Israelites to eat only unleavened bread as a remembrance of God's solidarity and strength. God then kept his promise to free the Israelites, allowing them to miraculously cross the Red Sea. Moses and his people were now on their way to the Promised Land. But soon after gaining their freedom, the Hebrews found themselves in a barren land. They grumbled to Moses and Aaron about their hunger. God responded to their pleas, as we read in the book of Exodus: "I am going to rain bread from heaven for you, and each day the people shall go out and gather enough for that day. In that way I will test them, whether they will follow my instruction or not" (16:4).

Here God again provides for their material food in the form of manna, a kind of bread. But God also offers them, and us, a spiritual lesson. God provides only enough manna for a given day, and no more. The lesson is that God wants the Israelites to be totally dependent on him—to have their eyes only on him, to place their trust only in God. In these passages, we see a God who tangibly provides both material bread and spiritual bread for the journey. This theme of bread as sustenance continues throughout the Old Testament, with many examples being offered by Solomon, Isaiah, and Hosea.

We see even more emphasis placed on bread in the New Testament. We are first introduced to the theme of bread as sustenance in the Gospels' description of Jesus's stay in the desert for forty days, when he fasted and prepared for his future ministry. Jesus permitted himself to experience a very real, physical hunger for food. Thus he came to know the same agony that his ancestors had known wandering in the desert. Satan's temptation of Christ, who was physically exhausted after forty days of fasting, was most cruel: "If you are the Son of God, command these stones to become loaves of bread" (Matt 4:3). Jesus opposed this irresistible, mouth-watering enticement of the edible bread by stating: "It is written, 'One does not live by bread alone but by every word that comes from the mouth of God'" (Matt 4:4). With his sole weapon a verse from the book of Deuteronomy, the starving victor beat the tempting enemy, and in so doing revealed the ancient biblical account of manna in the desert to be a prefiguring sign of his own life-giving bread.

Elsewhere in the New Testament, we witness the symbolism of bread when Jesus feeds over five thousand people. He miraculously multiplies the bread and fish to feed, again both spiritually and materially, the people of God.

In the simplest but greatest of all prayers, the Lord's Prayer, Jesus teaches us to depend on God for every blessing. We say, "Give us this day our daily bread" (Matt 6:11), again calling to mind the daily manna given to the wandering Israelites.

In the Gospel of John, Jesus states in the bluntest of terms, "I am the bread of life. Whoever comes to me will never be hungry, and whoever believes in me will never be thirsty" (John 6:35). What a profound mystery of faith and grace! Jesus did not say that he would *give* us or *show* us the bread of life, but that he *is* the bread of life.

During the harrowing days leading to his death, Jesus fulfilled his announcement that he is the bread of life. At the Last Supper, Jesus instituted the meal of bread and wine as his Body and Blood. The mystery of the Eucharist is unexplainable in words, yet expresses a most intimate connection to Christ and the body of believers. Eucharist itself means *thanksgiving*, and the Church now sets aside Sunday in particular to remember the spiritual and material blessings that God bestows upon us— especially the great blessing of the Incarnation and Resurrection of our Lord Jesus Christ.

Alexander Schmemann, a Christian pastor and theologian of the twentieth century, offers these words that still ring true in the twenty-first century. The author emphasizes the joyful and unifying strength of the Eucharist, as experienced in the Divine Liturgy:

> All is clear. All is simple and bright. Such fulness fills everything. Such joy permeates everything. Such love radiates through everything. We are again in the *beginning*, where our ascent to the table of Christ, in his kingdom, began. We depart into life, in order to witness and to fulfil our calling. Each has his own, but it is also our common ministry, common liturgy—"in the communion of the Holy Spirit." "Lord, it is good that we are here!"[5]

Sermons for Winter

A Baptismal Sermon

Today we will all be witnesses to the baptism of Michael Orlovsky. Actually, we will behold three sacraments: baptism, chrismation, and Michael's reception of the Eucharist for the first time. Thus at the conclusion of this service, which weaves together all three sacraments, Michael will be a full member of the Orthodox Church.

The service begins in the back of the sanctuary, wherein we offer a prayer of exorcism, which sounds rather dramatic. But one must first reject Satan before one can accept Christ. Thus Barbara, on behalf of Michael, will answer a series of questions: Do you reject Satan, and all his works, and all his worship, and all his pomp? Have you renounced Satan? Do you join Christ? Have you joined Christ?

By way of proving or professing faith in Christ, Barbara, on behalf of Michael, will read the Nicene Creed. The words of the Creed were written in the fourth century and have remained unchanged for 1700 years in the Orthodox Church. The Creed is a basic summary of the faith, outlining the three persons of the Trinity, the role of the Church, the reverence for Scripture, and other vital points.

After concluding this portion of the service, titled "the making of a catechumen," the priest, sponsor, and catechumen move to the front of the sanctuary, surrounding the font. Our faith understands Jesus to be perfect God and perfect man, and thus he had no reason to be baptized. Yet Jesus set an example for us to follow in all things, including baptism. The font calls to mind the Jordan River and the baptism of Jesus by John the Baptist.

Following a series of prayers, the catechumen is disrobed and wrapped in a white sheet and towel. He is anointed with the oil of gladness, immersed in the font three times, anointed with the holy chrism, and his hair is tonsured in the sign of the cross. Michael will then be redressed, this time in all-white clothes.

St. Paul, in his Letter to the Galatians, states that "as many of you as have been baptized into Christ have put on Christ" (3:27 KJV). St. Paul implies that once baptized, we become new creations in Christ. Thus the new clothes represent the reality of being a new creation in Christ. The white emphasizes wholeness, purity, and a new beginning.

After the newly illumined is fully dressed, we celebrate with a procession around the font three times, chanting the verse by St. Paul, "As many . . . as have been baptized in Christ, have put on Christ [Alleluia]." We then recite two readings from Scripture, Romans 6:3–11 and Matthew 28:16–20, both relating to baptism. Soon after the readings, Michael will proceed to the area before the altar and receive the Holy Eucharist for the first time. As we stated at the outset, following these three sacraments, Michael becomes a full member of the Orthodox Church.

Your role here today is not as innocent bystanders. As witnesses to this service, you have two main responsibilities. First, you are called to pray for Michael, that the seed of faith may be planted in his soul. Pray for his parents and sponsor that they may, with sincerity and earnestness, raise Michael in the Christian faith.

Your second responsibility begins tomorrow and continues into the future. You are called to be good role models and examples for Michael. You see, he is not being baptized as an individual. Rather, he is being baptized into the community of faith, the body of Christ. That means that all of us have a responsibility to assist Michael in his development and relationship with Christ.

> Jesus came and said to them, "All authority in heaven and on earth has been given to me. Go therefore and make disciples of all nations, baptizing them in the name of the Father and of the Son and of the Holy Spirit." (Matt 28:18–19)

Bringing Orthodoxy to America
(Sunday after Epiphany: Matthew 4:12–17)

In today's Gospel reading, Jesus officially begins his public ministry. His baptism completed, Jesus begins to fulfill the prophecy of Isaiah of bringing light to "the people who walked in darkness" (9:2). Similar to John the Baptist, Jesus's first official words in his public ministry are, "Repent, for the kingdom of heaven has come near" (Matt 4:17). Jesus begins to reach out to the public, making his gospel message available to everyone.

As a Church, we have a similar calling to bring the message of the good news to the world, to bring light to those in darkness, to fulfill a public ministry to those around us. But does the general population in America know what the Orthodox Church is? For a variety of reasons, the Orthodox Church here in America is basically a small and alien faith with a public relations problem. Some in this country ask if we are "almost Catholic." Others read the term *Orthodox* and label us as "Orthodox Jews."

If you really want to know what people in America think of the Orthodox faith, consider visiting the myriad of Internet chat rooms, blogs, and Web sites that host Orthodox dialogues. There you get an idea of what people think about our Church. One site in particular that I read this past week should be of interest to us. An Orthodox priest offered an online class to anyone interested in learning about the Orthodox faith. At the conclusion of the class, the priest administered a mock final exam, mostly for feedback purposes. The priest asked the following essay question: "How should the Orthodox faithful present their faith in today's American context?" The responses were quite interesting and varied.

One student wrote about the history of the Church, emphasizing the ability of the faithful to endure throughout the centuries. This person noted that this endurance is:

> a huge contribution that has been given to our society today. The Orthodox faith never gave up on what [it] believed in. It wouldn't take no as an answer. It was and forever will be a possible dream. So often in our society people are willing to give up and take a back seat of mediocrity. People need to look at

what the Orthodox did and have that as a reminder that with a mixture of hope and hard work, nothing can stop a dream from becoming a reality.

Along the same lines, another student wrote,

Orthodoxy should emphasize the longevity of the Church's existence despite persecution because it illustrates how strong faith is. This would be a major contribution to an American society that is plagued with depression. It demonstrates how this hope and trust is greater than any circumstance no matter how oppressive. The Orthodox saints did not seem to be depressed or sad about experiencing some difficulty because they knew there was something greater than the trouble around them.

Someone else concentrated on the teachings of the Orthodox Church, which have been guarded and transmitted faithfully from the beginnings of Christianity. She wrote,

The bishops act as proclaimer[s] of truth while all the people are guardians of the truth. I think it is important to note that the whole laity is involved in the faith and guarding it and not the clergy alone. It is not a democracy per se, but the people are involved in the faith and the proceedings surrounding it.

Another topic that was highlighted was the role that icons can play in sharing the faith with Americans:

As Presbyterians, my Church does not use icons, but I see them as a very powerful tool. For me, icons arouse emotions as well as provide a vision of the spiritual world. Any time I have ever seen an icon or even pictures of Churches with elaborate architecture, I was filled with awe. They can provide constant reminders of the faith and its history.

Finally, this student offered a perspective on Orthodox unity and diversity:

The Orthodox Church provides much diversity in worship, customs, and traditions. While the worship in the Orthodox Church in Russia may dictate that one stands still throughout the Liturgy, in the Churches in Africa the faithful sing loudly and even dance throughout their worship. Orthodoxy allows each follower to worship according to their native culture.

Many other comments were offered as a result of this online class. In summary, the perspective of these non-Orthodox students—the areas that might best speak to contemporary America—were the legacy of witness and martyrdom, the apostolic faith preserved faithfully for two thousand years, icons, and Orthodox unity and diversity.

Although the insights offered by the non-Orthodox students are helpful, the truth is that Americans will only become interested in Orthodoxy if they see the faith lived out in our lives and in our parishes. Theological and historical arguments will only go so far. The changed lives of Orthodox people will be what most inspires others to seek Orthodoxy. That is why Jesus's first word in his public ministry was the command to repent, meaning to change one's heart and to change one's direction toward Christ. When we as individuals and as a parish repent on a daily basis, only then will we see Orthodoxy grow in America.

Many of you know Bishop Gerasimos (Papadopoulos) of blessed memory. He was a gentle and wise man whose presence on the campus of Holy Cross School of Theology inspired us so much. He told us in one of his Bible studies that Orthodoxy is a young Church here in America, and that two things are still needed for us to grow. One is monasticism, and the other is martyrdom. He stated that historically, these two facets of the Church were necessary for growth and vibrancy. If there is one trait that underlies both monasticism and martyrdom, it is the word *repentance*. May we strive to fulfill the command of Jesus in today's Gospel reading to repent.

THE DESERT FATHERS AND MOTHERS

I n our modern and progressive society, we often view monasticism with great skepticism. People often wonder, "Why would anyone forego all the possibilities of fame, riches, and comfort for a life of poverty and masochism?" Yet the impact of monasticism on Church life is incalculable. The liturgical cycle of services, the hymns of the Church, and very many of the spiritual giants of Orthodoxy emerged from the monastic ranks. Thus a brief study of this topic is necessary to gain a deeper insight into the Orthodox faith.

Some form of monastic life existed from pre-Christian times; John the Baptist lived in a monastic community before becoming the forerunner of Christ. The formal presence of this disciplined life, however, appeared in the late third and early fourth centuries, when the hermits Anthony, Pachomius, and others fled to the arid and desolate deserts of Egypt. These ascetics practiced prayer, fasting, solitude, and simplicity as a means of developing an intense relationship with God. The Desert Fathers and Mothers, as they would soon be called, believed that striving for a life of purification in the desert would enable them to follow God's call in a deliberate and fruitful way. Soon the holiness and wisdom that emanated from these desert dwellers brought many men and women to search for illumination in this barren setting.

When Emperor Constantine experienced his dramatic conversion to Christianity in 312 AD, the Church persecutions drew to a close, and the faith slowly became a part of mainstream life in the empire. Yet the end of persecutions did not mean that the world had accepted the ideals of Christ—the world continued to prefer darkness to light. Many more people fled to the desert, wondering whether the members of the Church could occupy positions of influence in society without losing their moral integrity and independence.

These single-minded monastics cleansed and refined their focus on God through ascetic efforts, and soon pilgrims began to seek out their counsel. Some would accept visitors who were in need of healing and spiritual direction. One result of this desert movement was the simple, direct, and concrete sayings that contained words of wisdom. For example:

Abba Pambo asked Abba Anthony, "What ought I to do?" and the old man said to him, "Do not trust in your own righteousness, do not worry about the past, but control your tongue and your stomach."[6]

A brother said to St. Anthony, "Pray for me." The old man said to him, "I will have no mercy on you, nor will God have any, if you yourself do not make an effort and if you do not pray to God."[7]

Thousands of these pithy pieces of instruction remain with us to this day in written form. They need to be read, however, in context. These nuggets of wisdom are not abstract ideas, but were offered in particular situations. Although it is true that not all Christians are called to be monastics, we can state with assurance that all committed followers of Christ can integrate many of the practices and attitudes of the Desert Fathers and Mothers into their lives. Some of the ideals that capture the monastic wisdom are simplicity of life (freedom from attachments), the importance of silence and stillness in one's daily life, and prayer. St. Anthony once said,

He who sits in solitude and is quiet hath escaped from three wars: hearing, speaking, seeing: yet against one thing shall he continually battle: that is, his own heart.[8]

The teaching point of this axiom is that, as Christians, we are constantly bombarded by distractions—both internal and external stimuli. We learn about ourselves in silence, without distractions, when conscious and unconscious concerns of our souls surface.

The essence of spirituality in the desert was not taught but caught; it was a whole way of life. The Desert Fathers and Mothers did not have one systematic method or approach. Rather, they worked and strived to redirect every aspect of their bodies, minds, and souls to God. The writings and spirituality of these Fathers and Mothers continue to inspire and instruct Christian followers to the present age.

Someone asked Abba Anthony, "What must one do in order to please God?" The old man replied, "Pay attention to what I tell you: whoever you may be, always have God before your eyes; whatever you do, do it according to the testimony of the holy Scriptures; in whatever place you live, do not easily leave it. Keep these precepts and you will be saved."[9]

SUPER BOWL SUNDAY

Today is a high holy day. No, it is not Christmas or Pascha. Today is Super Bowl Sunday, a major feast day for those who follow the religion called football. Sarcasm aside, I wonder if there are a few parallels between the religion of football and the religion of Christianity. Below is a list of comparisons for your perusal.

First, the National Football League (NFL) has a team in most major cities in America. Each team is designated with a team name, like "the Jets" or "the Steelers." The Church, on the other hand, has communities scattered across the country, each with a specific name, such as "St. Nicholas" or "Annunciation."

Second, football teams play in massive stadiums, some seating eighty thousand faithful congregants. The stadiums are decorated with banners, advertising billboards, and an entertaining scoreboard. Our parishes meet in church buildings, where we sit in pews instead of box seats. The church sanctuary is decorated with icons, candles, and a cross, and colorful garments are worn by the priest.

Third, football teams have fight songs, sung especially loudly following a touchdown or great play. Fans sing in unison and act out hand and body gestures to emphasize their enthusiasm. Christians have hymns that praise God and remind us of the greatness of our Creator. Some congregations have chanters who sing a cappella, while others have choirs with organ accompaniment.

The NFL has a Hall of Fame in Canton, Ohio, where the stars of the past come to life. Game jerseys, video highlights, and other artifacts provide a living history of the sport. Our Church honors saints, the holy people of the past who are remembered for their virtues and service to God. We have icons, biographies, and relics that tell the story of these "all-stars."

The NFL has rituals that express the faith of its fans. There is tailgating before a game, subscription to team magazines, and the wearing of team jerseys with a favorite player's number. The Orthodox faith has rituals as well. We participate in worship services and sacraments as a way of growing in our journey with Christ. We wear crosses as a reminder of this faith in Jesus.

For devout football followers, there are shrines that are visited, much like a pilgrimage. People travel to Wisconsin in order to visit and touch the "frozen tundra" of Lambeau Field in Green Bay. Others create a shrine in their home to pay homage to their sporting heroes. Helmets, autographed game balls, and ticket stubs remind the faithful of their devotion to the team. Christians have shrines as well. We visit holy sites in Jerusalem or places where saints have lived. We have shrines in our homes, too—prayer corners where icons, candles, prayer ropes, holy water, the Bible, prayer books, and other items reinforce our commitment to Christ.

Have I taken this comparison between the religions of football and Christianity too far? I do not mean to demean athletics in general or football in particular. I also will be watching the game tonight with one billion other people. But I wonder if we as Christians have lost our balance or perspective on things. Why is it that we can memorize the career statistics of Peyton Manning but cannot remember a few verses from Scripture? Why is it that we can sit in the snow and rain for three hours watching a football game but balk at attending a church service at the first sign of a snowflake?

By all means, enjoy the game tonight. There is much to learn from athletics, such as teamwork, goal-setting, sacrifice, and many other positive attributes. But as Christians, we need to keep the big picture always at the forefront. Jesus reminds us to love God with all our heart, mind, soul, and strength. One hundred years from now, few will remember the winner of tonight's game. But one hundred years from now our souls will still be of great value—to us, and to God.

A Holy Self-Esteem

Self-esteem. This term has been one of the buzzwords of the last ten years. Sociologists and psychologists have cited statistics that 90% of Americans suffer from low self-esteem or a poor self-image. Dr. Phil, Oprah, Montel Williams, and others consider the impact that low self-esteem has on families and on society. Walk into any bookstore and you will find countless books in the self-help section on building a positive self-image.

School systems, court systems, and even communities of faith have wrestled with this question: "What can we do to raise people's self-esteem and to give them a more positive self-image?" Several suggestions have been proposed. In one book the author hints that if you stand in front of a mirror every morning and recite short, positive messages about how special you are, you will improve your self-esteem. A similar theory holds that we should do nothing to make others feel bad about themselves and, instead, do everything to make people feel good about themselves. By doing so, this theorist contends, our societies, our schools, and even our churches will be better places. Sounds great, doesn't it? The problem is, it's a lie.

Let's consider another approach. Jesus once told the story of two builders, one who built a house on sand and one who built a house on rock. We all know what happened: a storm came along, and the house built on sand was destroyed. Yet the house built on rock withstood the storm, because its foundation was secure. The lesson is simple: build your life on your relationship with Christ and you can be sure that, when faced with difficulties, you will be able to withstand the strain. The same lesson applies to self-image: build self-esteem on the truth of Jesus Christ, not on the sandy soil of popular psychology.

Another passage from the Gospel, the Parable of the Publican and the Pharisee, offers further proof of what Jesus wants us to understand about healthy self-image. When Jesus first told this parable, no one had ever heard the phrases "low self-esteem" or "positive self-image." But it doesn't take a psychiatrist to see who fits into which category. The Pharisee felt very good about himself (an overly positive self-image). You can almost see him as he marches into the temple for prayer—the way he carries himself and the way he wants to make sure everybody can hear his prayer. The Pharisees held a very high position in society and were well respected for their religious practices.

Yet Jesus points out that this Pharisee was building his life on the sandy soil of self-reliance, or self-importance. This Pharisee illustrates that the answer to the self-esteem issue is not simply feeling better about yourself. The Pharisee felt very good about himself but was not in a right relationship with God. Pride, arrogance, and self-importance lead us away from a healthy self-esteem. It is possible to become so self-centered that we exclude God and others.

The other person in the parable, the tax collector (or publican), was suffering from what we might call "low self-esteem." Tax collectors were despised by all in Jewish society. They often lined their own pockets by overcharging people on their taxes. While the people "oohed" and "aa-hed" at the Pharisees' righteousness, they might very well have spat in the face of the tax collector. It is easy to see why the tax collector may have felt poorly about himself. Yet the tax collector came before God with a humble spirit. You can feel the honesty in his voice as he prays, "God, have mercy on me!"

Amazingly, the man who technically did everything right religiously was the one who ultimately had no relationship with God. Yet the man who lived a sinful life, but admitted his fault, was heard by God and was forgiven. The example of the Pharisee highlights that what each of us needs is not higher self-esteem, but higher "God-esteem." Once we commit our lives to Christ, we must trust in his goodness and guidance. Doing so will lead us to experience a sense of self-worth that no psychologist or self-help book can ever foster. Feeling good about ourselves is no mirage: God created each person in his image, all the while offering unconditional love. All that is required from us is to accept this gift and respond to God's love by opening our lives to his presence.

> Trust in the Lord with all your heart, and do not rely on your own insight. In all your ways acknowledge him, and he will make straight your paths. (Prov 3:5–6)

MOTHER TERESA'S SPIRITUAL STRUGGLES

On the tenth anniversary of Mother Teresa's death, a new book on the correspondence that she had with her spiritual directors over the course of many decades was released. The book, entitled *Mother Teresa: Come Be My Light,* details the struggles of her spiritual life: the doubts, the inner loneliness, the vulnerabilities of the human condition that she experienced.

Consider two excerpts from her letters. Mother Teresa writes, "Jesus has a very special love for you . . . As for me—the silence and the emptiness is so great that I look and do not see, listen and do not hear."[10] Elsewhere she writes, "I am told that God lives in me—and yet the reality of darkness and coldness and emptiness is so great that nothing touches my soul."[11]

Critics of the book state that Mother Teresa is not the saint we think her to be, because these letters expose her weaknesses. They wonder how she could be a Christian champion by day and have such misgivings about Christ at night. Christopher Hitchens, a renowned atheist, went so far as to call Mother Teresa a fraud.

What are we, as practicing Christians, to make of such a book? Let's take a look at this issue from two perspectives.

First, the Christian life is a spiritual warfare, an unseen warfare. It is difficult to find any life of a saint or holy person that does not acknowledging the joys and struggles of the Christian life. Listen to the words of St. John of Kronstadt, a Russian parish priest of the nineteenth and early twentieth centuries:

> Do not fear spiritual conflict, do not flee it; where there is no struggle, there is no virtue; where faith and love are not tempted, one cannot be sure whether they really exist. They are proved and revealed in adversity, that is, in difficult and grievous circumstances, external or internal, in sickness, sorrow and privations.[12]

A careful reading of Scripture highlights the physical and spiritual sacrifices that many of God's faithful experienced. Eleven of the twelve apostles were martyred for the faith. St. Paul wrote that in his ministry he was shipwrecked, beaten, and left half-dead countless times (2 Cor 11:23–27). And did not Jesus himself undergo spiritual abandonment in the Garden of Gethsemane?

But my favorite scriptural comparison to this Mother Teresa quotation is found in the Psalms. The author of the Psalms was a devout lover of God, yet consider these words of darkness and discouragement:

> How long, O Lord? Will you forget me forever? How long will you hide your face from me? How long must I bear pain in my soul, and have sorrow in my heart all day long? . . . Consider and answer me, O Lord my God! (Ps 13:1–3)

I submit to you that every faithful and holy person who has lived in this fallen world has experienced dryness and desolation in his or her spiritual life. Thus the first point that I would like to make is that the Christian life is a spiritual warfare, an unseen warfare.

My second point regarding this book on Mother Teresa is that she sought spiritual direction and counsel. Built into the life of any committed Christian is spiritual accountability; no one can truly grow in the faith without periodic confession and spiritual direction. Left to our own discretion, we can create our own theology and justify every thought and action in our lives, and this is ideal ammunition for the devil. Mother Teresa, true to her faith, sought regular spiritual counsel for objectivity, support, and reassurance.

I believe that this book on Mother Teresa's letters will only enhance her status as a holy servant of God. Despite her vulnerabilities and doubts, she selflessly provided for those in need and inspired millions to seek Christ and serve others.

Before closing this reflection, I want to return to Psalm 13, from which I quoted the dark and lonely passage above. But this time I want to present the entire psalm, which begins with despair in the first few verses but ends with the ultimate victory that God provides:

> How long, O Lord? Will you forget me forever? How long will you hide your face from me? How long must I bear pain in my soul, and have sorrow in my heart all day long? How long shall my enemy be exalted over me?
>
> Consider and answer me, O Lord my God! Give light to my eyes, or I will sleep the sleep of death, and my enemy will say, "I have prevailed"; my foes will rejoice because I am shaken.

But I trusted in your steadfast love; my heart shall rejoice in your salvation. I will sing to the Lord, because he has dealt bountifully with me.

ASTROLOGY: AN ORTHODOX PERSPECTIVE

A question that is often posed to parish priests is, "What is the Church's opinion about astrology?" Moreover, a follow-up question usually is, "Can I be a practicing Christian and still enjoy astrology?" Perhaps we can use this opportunity to outline the Orthodox position on this topic.

The Judeo-Christian understanding of astrology clearly submits that there is a distinction between creation and the Creator. For Orthodox Christians, this precept is affirmed in the first verse of the Nicene Creed: "I believe in one God, the Father Almighty, Creator of heaven and earth, and of all things visible and invisible." The Church also teaches that we are created by the love of God and that we are most fully human when we love God and each other.

The second greatest gift that God has given to each human being, after life itself, is free choice, or free will. We have the ability to make choices in life, even the capacity to accept or reject God's love.

The dictionary definition of astrology is "the divination of the supposed influences of the stars and planets on human affairs and terrestrial events by their positions and aspects."[13] Astrologers predict future trends and developments that directly affect a person. Supposedly, the relationship between the stars determines what kind of personality traits one will have and how that person's life will play out.

St. Gregory the Great a sixth-century hierarch, responded to the credibility of astrology. He writes,

> In Persia, when a child is born to a king and becomes a prince, they say his star caused it to be so; but then he asks, who can estimate how many slaves were born at the same time and moment as the king's son? And yet the sons of kings, born in the same hour as the slaves, go on to a kingdom, while slaves born together with them die in slavery.[14]

Astrology asserts that human freedom is limited, subject to independent and subjective forces beyond our control. The Orthodox Church rejects such terms as *fate* and *destiny* precisely because these notions deny our freedom, our self-determination, and the transforming power of God.

From the beginning of Church history, astrology has been viewed as a form of idolatry, since one's belief in the stars is placed above God's power and creative force. It was condemned as early as the second century in a book entitled the *Didache* (also called *The Teaching of the Twelve Apostles*). Several centuries later, the Blessed Augustine "[felt] that anyone who believes that our loving God would give power to stars in order to direct and govern our lives offends God's mercy and love."[15]

It is not difficult to see why the Church rejects the field of astrology—it denies the transforming and caring presence of God. In place of the glorious freedom of humans presented to us in the Christian faith, astrology claims that mechanical and deterministic forces beyond our control govern our lives.

This ancient tale might put fate and destiny in perspective:

There was an army general who decided to attack his country's enemy even though his soldiers were outnumbered ten to one. The general was sure he could win, but his soldiers were full of doubt. On the way to battle the general announced, "I shall now toss a coin. If it is heads, we shall win. If tails, we shall lose. Destiny will now reveal herself." He tossed the coin; it was heads. The soldiers were so eager to fight that they wiped out the opposition. The next day the general's assistant said to the general, "No one can change destiny!" "Quite right," replied the general with a smile, showing him a coin that was heads on both sides. Which begs the question, who makes destiny?[16]

THE MYSTERY OF SUFFERING

One of the most powerful verses in Scripture is found at the beginning of Psalm 22. The psalmist writes:

My God, my God, why have you forsaken me? Why are you so far from helping me, from the words of my groaning? O my God, I cry by day, but you do not answer; and by night, but find no rest. (vv. 1–2)

Many of the victims of Hurricane Katrina may now be expressing these same feelings of pain. Tragedy comes in different shades, but the common denominator is human suffering. Whether they are immediately due to the attacks on September 11, the tsunami in Asia, or the famine in Sudan, pain and suffering are part of the human condition.

The Judeo-Christian tradition teaches us that God did not create evil, suffering, or death, yet he allows these phenomena to occur. If God is love, then why does he permit evil? The short answer is: God gives human beings the ability to make choices in life so that we may freely choose to enter into relationship with him. Unfortunately, this human free will can result in either good or evil consequences.

Some may ask, "Couldn't God have foreseen this potential for pain, suffering, and death?" No doubt he did. But consider this: many of us are parents. Even before we bore children, could we not foresee the real possibility that our kids could suffer disappointment or pain or heartache in life? Of course we did—yet we still had children. Why? Because we knew there was also the potential for tremendous joy and deep love and great meaning in relationships. The same is true in God's creative plan.

Please do not misunderstand me. I am not offering trite answers to the mystery of suffering. No response to this dilemma can ever be satisfactory or convincing. Personally, I rarely ask why God allows suffering. I am more amazed by how people successfully deal with pain and suffering; I am astounded when I see individuals overcome and transfigure their painful circumstances. The Lance Armstrongs and Nelson Mandelas of the world come to mind. I am equally sure that each person in this church knows of someone who has experienced pain, suffering, or injustice and, through God's grace, transformed it into something for the greater good.

For Christians, the healing power of God is always within reach. In Scripture and in the lives of saints, we read countless examples of people who experience pain, sorrow, and suffering. We then read how the God of compassion, the God of reassurance, the God of healing manifests himself in the midst of this suffering.

Perhaps it is worthwhile to highlight a more modern example. There is a passage in Jim Forest's book, entitled *The Ladder of the Beatitudes*, that I will share with you:

> I think of friends of ours, Tom and Glinda Johnson-Medland, who for seven years prayed for a child and finally conceived one only to see her die before birth. "I became furious with God," Tom recalls, "and felt totally betrayed. If this was how God treated his friends . . ."
>
> Fortunately the priest Tom turned to in the midst of his rage and grief had good advice. "I don't care how angry you are at God," the priest said, "just get into Church every week and take the mother of God some flowers. Stand in front of her icon, or kneel there, or roll around on the floor—I don't care. Scream, yell, cry, curse, I don't care, but go and be with her. She is the mother of our Lord, and she knows. She understands the loss of a child. Will you promise me you will do that? And take Glinda with you as often as she can go."
>
> There was no false piety in the priest's advice, no glib slogans about God's inscrutable will or how happy they ought to be that their child was in heaven. Instead, he sent Tom and Glinda to Christ's mother, who herself was made a refugee by Herod, saw her Son condemned, saw nails hammered through his limbs, stood at the foot of the cross, and took part in his burial.
>
> Tom kept his promise. Most of the time, laying flowers on the icon, he was in tears. "Tears gushed from deep in me. I was tapping into a sorrow I did not know, unleashing emotions I had never dreamed possible."
>
> Glinda, herself a therapist, says that for months she often felt close to losing her sanity.
>
> Tom and Glinda's grieving was long and painful, yet some-how the weekly gift of flowers to the mother of God helped them. "She became," Tom says, "our sweetness and our health, a meadow with softening flowers, our tears in the cleansing path

of sorrow, our nurse in times of sickness, our mother when we needed to be held."

Looking back two years later, Glinda said that her experience taught her that "mourning creates transparency in people. It tells people that we are in pain and that we have experienced some type of loss. It opens us up for others to know."[17]

I have no concluding or summary statement to offer. This sensitive topic must always be left open ended. But consider this: the author of Psalm 22, the passage I opened with, knew firsthand the anguish of this world. He felt comfortable expressing his pain to God. Although the first two verses of the psalm convey pain and suffering, the end of the poem is filled with hope and trust. The psalmist writes,

All the ends of the earth shall remember and turn to the Lord; and all the families of the nations shall worship before him. For dominion belongs to the Lord, and he rules over the nations.

Posterity will serve him; future generations will be told about the Lord, and proclaim his deliverance to a people yet unborn. (vv. 27–28, 30–31)

FASTING

I f there is one topic in Church circles that draws the greatest variance of opinion, it is fasting. Ask ten practicing Christians how they fast (or *if* they fast), and you will receive twelve responses. It is easier to dialogue about one's favorite passage from Scripture, or one's favorite hymn or feast day. A discussion on fasting, however, often leads to strong opinions or blank stares. However, since fasting is prevalent in the liturgical life of Orthodox Christians, we may want to consider its importance in our daily journey. The fact that Jesus fasted before beginning his three-year public ministry, and before every major decision, should give us pause to consider integrating this spiritual tool into our own arsenal. Let us first consider fasting in a wider context: the reasons *why* people fast.

First, people fast for ecological reasons. Environmentalists recognize the limitations of our food supply. Oftentimes we don't appreciate the gift of food and all that it takes to grow, cultivate, and distribute food worldwide.

Second, people fast for political reasons. Mahatma Gandhi, Martin Luther King, Jr., Nelson Mandela, and countless others attempted to make statements regarding the social causes of their day through fasting. Others would join in the fast as an expression of solidarity and commitment.

Third, people fast for health reasons. One cannot pick up a daily newspaper without reading about the obesity epidemic that threatens the U.S. and other developed nations. In order to control blood pressure, cholesterol, and heart disease, people attempt to fast to ensure a healthy present and future.

What is interesting is that when people fast for ecological, political, or health reasons, few bat an eye as to fasting's purpose and strength. Yet when our Church cultivates a need for spiritual growth through the practice of fasting, many view the discipline as masochistic or anachronistic; we hear, "Fasting has nothing to do with my relationship with Christ."

Perhaps a brief focus on some passages from Scripture can illustrate the reasons why God's people fast.

First, God's people fast to lament their sins. In Deuteronomy, Moses fasted because of Israel's rebelliousness and sin:

> Then I lay prostrate before the Lord as before, forty days and forty nights; I neither ate bread nor drank water, because of all the sin you had committed, provoking the Lord by doing what was evil in his sight. For I was afraid that the anger that the Lord bore against you was so fierce that he would destroy you. But the Lord listened to me that time also. (Deut 9:18–19)

Today when we sin, we often shrug our shoulders and say, "Oh, sorry, Lord" and move on with our lives.

Second, God's people fast when a problem or concern arises. In the Old Testament when Esther put her life at risk to save the Jewish people from the evil Haman, advisor to King Ahasuerus, she instructed the faithful, "Go, gather all the Jews to be found in Susa, and hold a fast on my behalf, and neither eat nor drink for three days, night or day. I and my maids will also fast as you do" (Est 4:16).

When Daniel was thrown into the lion's den for praying to God, King Darius fasted on his behalf to save him from certain death:

> The king said to Daniel, "May your God, whom you faithfully serve, deliver you!" A stone was brought and laid on the mouth of the den, and the king sealed it with his own signet and with the signet of his lords . . . Then the king went to his palace and spent the night fasting; no food was brought to him. (Dan 6:16–18)

When we have a problem, do we consider fasting as an avenue toward resolving it? When fasting, we clear away all distractions. We are more open to God's guidance and direction. Our anxiety levels decrease, so we make more healthy and wise decisions in life.

Third, God's people fast in order to prepare. As noted earlier, Jesus fasted in the desert and *then* began his three-year public ministry. In the Gospel of St. Luke, the prophetess Anna fasted while waiting in the temple to receive the infant Jesus. In the Acts of the Apostles, the Church community fasted over Paul and Barnabas before they were sent out to evangelize and begin the work of the Lord. In every scriptural case, fasting was used as a tool to know God better and to deepen one's relationship with him.

Make a new commitment to fasting, knowing that for centuries God's people have used this spiritual prescription to receive God's grace and wisdom.

Jesus rebuked the demon, and it came out of him; and the child was cured from that very hour. Then the disciples came to Jesus privately and said, "Why could we not cast it out?" So Jesus said to them, "Because of your unbelief; for assuredly, I say to you, if you have faith as a mustard seed, you will say to this mountain, 'Move from here to there,' and it will move; and nothing will be impossible for you. However, this kind does not go out except by *prayer and fasting*." (Matt 17:18–21 NKJV, emphasis added)

SERMONS FOR SPRING

THE MARATHON RUNNER (LENT)

The scene is the 1968 Summer Olympics in Mexico City. A few thousand spectators remain in the Olympic stadium. It is late in the evening as the last of the marathon runners are carried off in exhaustion to first aid stations. The winner of the marathon had finished earlier in the evening, looking as fresh as when he started as he moved powerfully past the finish line.

As the remaining spectators prepare to leave, sirens and police whistles suddenly fill the muggy air. Confused, the spectators look toward the tunnel leading into the arena. There, entering the stadium, is a lone figure wearing the colors of Tanzania. His name is John Akhwari; he is the last man to finish the marathon. His leg is bloody and bandaged, and he grimaces with each step. He had severely injured his leg during the race. With great difficulty, Akhwari hobbles around the 400-meter track.

The remaining spectators rise and applaud the courage and commitment of this man as if they were receiving the winner. Akhwari painfully completes the run by crossing the finish line. Then he slowly walks off the field, barely acknowledging the cheering crowd.

Later, when asked why he had not quit, knowing his task was so painful and he had no chance for victory, Akhwari stated, "My country did not send me seven thousand miles to *start* the race. They sent me seven thousand to *finish* it."

This narrative is symbolic of our journey through the Lenten season. We begin with great promise, excited to tackle the disciplines and challenges of Lent. But as we travel on this six-week marathon, we begin to tire; we grimace with each step. We may even convince ourselves to give up along the way.

Fortunately, the Church offers many opportunities for us to strengthen ourselves for the long journey. With determination and fortitude like those of John Akhwari, we too can keep our focus, guided by the wisdom of the faith. Let us review several of the spiritual tools available to us during Lent.

The liturgical cycle of services during the Lenten season, in addition to the Sunday Divine Liturgy, provides a rudder for our trek; specifically, Great Compline, the Presanctified Liturgy, and the Akathist offer us much guidance:

> **Great Compline**—This evening service in which the sanctuary is dimly lit is often offered on the Mondays of Lent. Many Psalm readings and prayers lead the worshipper to experience the themes of repentance, forgiveness, and our dependence on God.

> **Pre-Sanctified Liturgy**—This evening Eucharistic service, offered on the Wednesdays (and Fridays) of Lent, features Old Testament readings that relate to and prefigure the life of Christ. The Eucharist, consecrated the previous Sunday, is an additional invitation to receive the Sacrament more frequently during Lent.

> **The Akathist to the Theotokos**—This evening service, offered on the Fridays of Lent, is a profound devotional poem dedicated to the Mother of God. Since the Feast of the Annunciation is often celebrated in the middle of the Lenten season (March 25), this poem becomes an especially powerful reminder of the miracle and mystery of the Incarnation of Christ.

In addition to participating in the liturgical rhythm of Lent, we can take many practical steps to fully invest ourselves in the preparation of Holy Week and the joyous celebration of Pascha. Ideally, we should seek the counsel of a spiritual father who can customize an appropriate blueprint for our journey. However, here are a few basic spiritual disciplines for us to consider:

- Purchase an Orthodox prayer book that you can refer to each day during Lent. Find a time clear of distractions to read selections of morning, afternoon, or evening prayers.

- Recite the Jesus Prayer (Lord Jesus Christ, Son of God, have mercy on me) at various intervals of the day. This helps us to remember the presence of God consistently.

- Prepare for the sacrament of confession by reading instructions and hints from available prayer books. Concentrate especially on ways in which your life and faith intersect: a problem that may be upsetting you, a question about the faith you may be struggling with, even the joys and blessings of your life.

- With the assistance of your spiritual father, determine an appropriate fasting discipline for Lent.

- Nurture yourself by preparing to receive the Eucharist on Sundays and Wednesdays (and Fridays, if possible).

- Attend a Lenten retreat in your area, during which you will learn more about the Orthodox faith and meet other committed Christians.

- Read books and/or articles on the lives of saints.

- Lent is not simply about your spiritual development and progress. Use this time to assist others in need by donating time and resources.

By incorporating these disciplines and practices into our Lenten journey, we will experience a closer relationship with Christ, other fellow Christians, and all those around us. As we revel in the light of the resurrected Christ on the night of Pascha, we will be able to mirror the words of marathoner John Akhwari and say within our hearts:

Christ did not give me this Lenten season to start. He gave me this Lenten season to finish!

KEEPING FAITH AND LENT

Frank Schaeffer converted to Orthodoxy some years ago and is a noted author and speaker on the faith. His recent book, however, entitled *Keeping Faith*, is not about the Christian faith, but about a father-son relationship. The story begins as Frank Schaeffer's son enters United States Marine Corp boot camp at Paris Island, and the body of the book is a series of letters, written back and forth by both the father and son, that chronicles the intense four-month period of boot camp. At times the letters are honest and funny, and usually they are very profound and moving.

The book does not glorify war, yet it offers a personal and first-hand perspective into what it means to be a soldier. More importantly for the Christian reader, the book offers parallel themes regarding the Lenten season: discipline, perseverance, concern for others, sacrifice, and aiming for a goal. Allow me to share several passages from this book and offer observations from an Orthodox point of view.

> Training started intense and slow. We recruits had been demoted to being toddlers who had to relearn everything. Nothing we knew was right. We did not know how to put on socks or tie our shoes. We did not know how to shower or shave . . . We thought we knew but our knowledge was a stumbling block, worse than nothing, civilian . . . We could not move into the next part of training until we completed each element (no matter how small), to the satisfaction of the Drill Instructors.[18]

Similarly, the elementary aspects of Lent include simplifying and prioritizing our lives. The contemporary society in which we live often distracts us from what is most vital—an intimate relationship with Christ. Lent can be a point of departure for relearning the fundamental components of our faith. The additional worship services, including Great Compline, Pre-Sanctified Liturgy, and the Akathist Hymn, offer a liturgical stepping stone for spiritual growth. Personal prayer, fasting, participation in the sacraments, and almsgiving build on the principles of Lent.

> As training days pass, a recruit's motivation to perform comes not from a desire to succeed as an individual, but from a desire

for the good of the whole platoon, the only people who truly understand him and would die for him at any moment. The brotherhood of the platoon is what makes life on Paris Island bearable. Training ceases to be an individual challenge. It must be done as a group, or it becomes meaningless and worthless.[19]

The *greater good* is the theme of this passage, and it applies to both the Marines and all of us in the Church body. The Lenten journey is not an individualistic program designed to attain our own selfish aspirations. Rather, the by-product of this season is that we are more aware of and compassionate toward the world around us. This principle is not limited to the Lenten season. Each opportunity to receive the Eucharist is an expression of our unity not only with Christ, but with each member of the body of Christ.

> As we moved into the last days of training, life on Paris Island finally made sense to us. The seemingly petty discipline that had been forced down our throats so hard through everything we did was no longer pointless busywork but an essential part of our daily boot camp lives. We began to understand why each individual task we were given, whether in the chow hall or the barracks, or even how we got dressed or were told to sit made sense. We saw how each detail of training contributed to being prepared for the larger challenges, how learning to think as a unit in the small things contributed to cohesiveness in the big ones.[20]

I remember spending time as a child during Lent and Holy Week with my grandmother. She was a pious woman who took me along to all the Church services and who followed the fasting guidelines of the faith very strictly. As deeply as I loved and respected her, I would often dread visiting her during Lent, knowing that the ascetical demands of the Church were quite stringent.

It was only years later that I realized the necessity of putting together the various building blocks of the faith. It was then that my grandmother's Lenten practices began to make sense. The disciplines of the Church were not for punishment's sake, but in order to make us strive toward a higher calling, a deeper connection with God.

Later in the book, John Schaeffer completes the four-month boot camp, having been truly transformed through the experience. He writes something interesting: when he returns to "the world," he finds that the lessons learned at Paris Island are not truly appreciated by civilians. During camp, he grew in discerning what discipline, perseverance, sacrifice, and concern for others truly meant, and in the end he discovered that he did not want to go back to the way he was before enlisting. The same should be true about our Lenten journey. We hope to be transformed in some way and to not want to be the way we were before.

Although our goal as Christians is quite different than the goals of those who join the Marines, St. Paul draws an image of what it means to be a soldier for Christ:

> Stand therefore, and fasten the belt of truth around your waist, and put on the breastplate of righteousness. As shoes for your feet put on whatever will make you ready to proclaim the gospel of peace. With all of these, take the shield of faith, with which you will be able to quench all the flaming arrows of the evil one. Take the helmet of salvation, and the sword of the Spirit, which is the word of God . . . Peace be to the whole community, and love with faith, from God the Father and the Lord Jesus Christ. (Eph 6:14–17, 23)

A REFLECTION ON THE HOLY CROSS
(THIRD SUNDAY OF LENT)

Let us take a journey together, back to a bleak, dark day in the year 33 AD when three men were led to a hilltop outside Jerusalem and crucified there. All three were sentenced for political conspiracy. Two of them had been brought to Jerusalem and speedily sentenced. The third man, Jesus of Nazareth, was accused of leading a dangerous political party. After an absurd trial, the Jewish leaders declared Jesus guilty of blasphemy, pretending to be the Son of God, and claiming to be God himself. Because those guilty of this offense were subject to the death penalty, Jesus was turned over to the Romans for sentencing and execution.

First, the three prisoners were stripped and severely whipped with lashes set with little pieces of bone and metal. The victims could barely stand after such a flogging. Since word had it that one of the criminals claimed to be a king, they took him, placed a red Roman cloak around his shoulders, thrust a reed into his hands, and pushed a crown of thorns down upon his head. Then, mocking him, they pretended to pay homage to him. Finally, he was led with the other two out of the Praetorium and up the narrow street to Golgotha, also known as the Place of the Skull.

As an added indignity, the three men were forced to carry the heavy crossbeams of their own crosses up the steep hill to the place of crucifixion. Weak from the constant beatings, they often needed help along the way. One of the prisoners fell three times, and a bystander, Simon of Cyrene, was pressed into service to help him.

On Golgotha the three upright sections of the crosses stood awaiting the cross beams and their victims. The prisoners were stripped of clothing, then fastened onto the crossbeams by nails driven through their hands. The beams were hoisted and attached to the uprights; the feet of each man were nailed to a projection jutting from it. Finally, a sign was hung above Jesus's head that bore the crime for which he was being executed. The curious crowd pressed very close, pushing, jeering, and taunting the condemned prisoners. The clothes of the dying fell to the soldiers, who divided some of them and cast lots for the better pieces.

Crucifixions were usually noisy and violent. The pain was excruciating, and often the crucified screamed and cursed and cried out. The condemned men on the two outside crosses were no exception. They cursed everyone and everything, and even took verbal shots at the prisoner on the central cross. Hours went by. It was this, the almost unending agony, that made crucifixion such a dread torture. Sometimes the victims would linger three or four days, dying minute by minute. They would actually suffocate to death as the raised position of the arms prevented the ribs from expanding to draw in air.

The person who hung from the center cross was different from most crucified criminals. He didn't scream and curse and bellow like a wounded bull. For the first few hours he hung there silently, patiently, a quiet dignity about him. There was no doubt about the pain he suffered; his face portrayed that. But he didn't give way to it or allow the agony to undo him.

If ever anyone had cause to be bitter and curse humankind, it was Jesus as he hung from the cross. His essential will and desire had been to bring human beings a deeper knowledge of God, to enable them to find the key to authentic living by loving God and one another. And this was how Jesus was rewarded—with crucifixion. And how did he respond? With nothing but love. From the four Gospels, we know that Jesus spoke only seven times from the cross, and each of these expressions reflected love. He cared for his detractors even though they crucified him. He made the cross a symbol of love by pouring forth a healing spring of divine concern when most people would have cried out in bitterness and anger or simply screamed in agony.

Some of his statements were so unusual that some people thought he might be deranged. He said, "Father, forgive them; for they do not know what they are doing" (Luke 23:34). In replying to the question of one of the men being crucified with him, he said, "Today you will be with me in Paradise" (Luke 23:43). He looked down upon his mother and his disciple John and said, "'Woman, here is your son.' Then he said to the disciple, 'Here is your mother'" (John 19:26–27). He was silent for a long period and then cried out, "My God, my God, why have you forsaken me?" (Matt 27:46; Mark 15:33).

At some point he cried out, "I am thirsty" (John 19:28). This was a common complaint for the crucified. The loss of blood caused a traumatic thirst that was almost unbearable. Someone soaked a sponge in wine and offered him a drink. At about three that afternoon, Jesus cried out, "It is finished" (John 19:30) and, "Father, into your hands I commend my spirit" (Luke 23:46). After that he spoke no more.

These are the cold, hard facts of what happened on the Friday just before the Passover Sabbath during the priesthood of Caiaphas. Is this the end of the story? If it were, Good Friday would be the most tragic day of all days, and there would be no Church or Christian faith. Good Friday is meaningless without the event that happened two days later, on the Sunday of Pascha.

But today our focus is not on the Resurrection of Christ, but on his Crucifixion. Why does the Church, on the third Sunday of Lent, direct our attention to the cross and Crucifixion of Christ? What is so important about this particular event that it is worth using our imagination to rediscover what happened on Golgotha? Why should we spend hours poring over every detail of this ghastly act of terror?

The response is something like this: the cross of Christ, when we are willing to face it, first strips us of our complacency. It then leads us to make a choice between a life of futility and a life of hope and ultimate victory. Some people today claim to accept Christ's ethical teachings yet deny his divinity. In response to this way of thinking, C. S. Lewis, the great twentieth-century Christian writer, writes this challenging statement on the meaning of the cross:

> A man who was merely a man and said the sort of things Jesus said would not be a great moral teacher. He would either be a lunatic . . . or else he would be the Devil of Hell. You must make your choice. Either this man was, and is, the Son of God: or else a madman or something worse.[21]

For those who do accept Jesus as the Messiah, the cross represents God's love for all people. God cared enough to endure even crucifixion to reveal his love for each one of us. Christ preached love—he taught it, he lived it, he died it. Christianity is not a collection of truths to be believed or laws to be obeyed. Christianity is a Person. Christianity is Christ.

St. Mary of Egypt and Repentance
(Fifth Sunday of Lent)

A wise person from centuries ago once said this about himself:

I was a revolutionary when I was young and all my prayer to God was, "Lord, give me the energy to change the world."

As I approached middle age and realized that half my life was gone without my changing a single soul, I changed my prayer to, "Lord, give me the grace to change all those who come in contact with me. Just my family and friends, and I shall be satisfied."

Now that I am an old man and my days are numbered, my one prayer is, "Lord, give me the grace to change myself. If I had prayed for this right from the start I should not have wasted my life."[22]

On the fifth Sunday of Lent, the Church celebrates the life of St. Mary of Egypt. In her lifetime she did not change the world, nor did she change her family or friends. Rather, by changing herself, she has become for all Christians a symbol of repentance.

St. Mary was a young woman in the sixth century who went to Alexandria and became a prostitute for many years. One day she was intrigued by a group of pilgrims traveling to Jerusalem to visit the Church of the Holy Resurrection. She went with them and, while in Jerusalem, was moved by a profound awareness of her own sinfulness. More importantly, she became aware of how far removed she was from God. She immediately repented and decided to change her life, living her remaining years in asceticism and prayer.

Much more can be said regarding the details of her life, but the example of St. Mary invites us to consider two questions: first, what is repentance; and second, why would someone repent?

In response to the first question, repentance, or *metanoia*, is a genuine conversion of mind and heart—a reorientation, a new outlook on one's self, on others, and on God. Sometimes repentance is immediate, but most of the time repentance is a gradual process. To illustrate this process, I will share with you an account of a modern-day St. Mary.

As a young priest, I was assigned as a chaplain to a state hospital that housed a substance abuse rehabilitation program. This center focused on group and individual counseling for its patients. I offered a group on spiritual resources available for rehabilitation. It was during one of these group meetings that I learned a new perspective on the meaning of repentance. As the members of the group introduced themselves one by one, I heard Gloria's story. I could tell almost immediately that she was an unusual person. Throughout the group discussion I sensed a joyful spirit, a hopefulness, from Gloria. After each of the group sessions ended, I would invite anyone who wished, to meet for individual counseling. This allowed the person an opportunity to share more in a confidential setting, since each person's needs were unique.

Gloria was one of those who came forward and placed her name on the list to meet privately. She shared her incredibly painful story with me. She was a cocaine addict who, in the midst of her addiction, turned to prostitution in order to support her drug habit. She had recently discovered that she was HIV positive. Gloria held nothing back as she conveyed the emotional pain and suffering in her life.

As Gloria was speaking I was struck by her gentleness and hopefulness. She exuded a sense of peacefulness, a trait not usually found in people at a detoxification center. At one point I asked her, "How do you remain so positive, so joyful?" She replied, "My mother has never given up on me. She loves me more than anyone else in the world." Later she added, "I know that God loves me and has never given up on me."

Gloria, in the midst of so much darkness and despair, experienced unconditional love through her mother. This love not only consoled her, but motivated her to change. Sometimes we think that repentance is simply a decision to change our minds and our actions. It is, but what else motivates that change? For Gloria, and for others, it is the experience of receiving unconditional love that leads us to the second question we posed earlier: why would someone repent?

A person might consider repenting out of fear or guilt or shame. From that perspective, however, God is viewed as harsh and judgmental. Such a relationship with God usually leads to bitterness and resentment. But what St. Mary of Egypt and Gloria teach us is that God is continually stretching his arms out in love, never forcing himself on us, but always waiting, always hoping that his children will return so that he can speak words of love to us. St. Mary and Gloria reveal to us that God has no desire to punish us—we've already punished ourselves by our waywardness. God wants only to offer his gift of love to us. God's only desire is to bless us.

A PARADE (PALM SUNDAY)

The year 1969 was a magical year in my youth. I attended four parades that year: in January, the New York Jets' Super Bowl victory parade; in August, a parade in honor of the Apollo 11 space mission's moon landing; in October, the New York Mets' World Series victory parade; and in November, the Thanksgiving Macy's Day Parade.

But out of all the parades I attended that year, the celebration welcoming the Apollo 11 astronauts back to earth included the widest variety of groups in attendance:

First were those who came simply to party. The event was an excuse to drink and become rowdy. This group had no interest in the accomplishments of the Apollo crew.

Second were those who picketed, believing that spending millions of dollars to send astronauts to the moon was a waste of resources. In their opinion, this money would have been better spent on the underprivileged in our own country.

Third were those who profited from the parade. Souvenirs, banners, hot dogs, and everything else you could imagine were sold to the crowds at the parade.

Fourth were the police and other security personnel. New York's finest were on horses controlling the mobs of people. Even within the procession there were armed forces keeping the proceedings safe for the masses.

Fifth were those who were amazed at the success of fulfilling President John F. Kennedy's goal to send astronauts to the moon and return them safely to the earth.

On this day—Palm Sunday—nearly two thousand years ago, another parade was celebrated. It featured Jesus of Nazareth, who was being welcomed into Jerusalem after a tumultuous three-year ministry. As Jesus processed through the streets, there was a wide variety of onlookers: people with their own agendas, their own perspectives. Let's revisit the groups who were at that parade:

First were the curious, who had heard about Lazarus being raised from the dead only the day before. These were probably people who were interested in seeing another miracle or magic trick, more interested in the gifts than the giver, more interested in being entertained than in getting to know Jesus.

Second were the twelve apostles, who were perhaps feeling powerful and important as their leader was hailed as a mighty hero. These same apostles would flee from Christ later in the week.

Third were the members of the Sanhedrin, or Jewish leaders, who felt threatened by Jesus. The Pharisees, scribes, and the other rabbis saw the hordes of people leaving the temple and following this charismatic "heretic," who called himself equal to God.

Fourth were Pontius Pilate and the Roman legions, who were leery of this personality who was causing disruptions and near riots.

Fifth were the true believers, who witnessed the teachings, the miracles, the healings, the sincerity, the courage, and the love of Jesus.

So you see, people come to parades for a variety of reasons. By the same token, people come to church for a variety of reasons as well. So who came to the Palm Sunday parade today? Why are people in church today?

Some came because they felt obligated to put in their time, to pacify God or members of their family, or they came out of force of habit.

Some came who may be skeptics, who wonder about this person of Jesus just as much as the people at that first Palm Sunday parade. Or maybe some are casual observers who are safely standing at a distance?

Some are here who are committed to serve Christ, to follow Christ, and to keep growing in their relationship with him.

Whatever category you may fit in, please remember this: the invitation to this parade, and the events of Holy Week, are extended to everyone. Christ does not require a perfect and complete faith. He does ask for an open heart, a willing spirit, and that our first step be taken in faith. After that initial step, Jesus will lead us to experience the events of this week in an intimate and life-changing manner. Come and see!

THE PASSOVER SEDER (PALM SUNDAY)

On the first Palm Sunday some two thousand years ago, countless numbers of Jews had already arrived in Jerusalem to celebrate the Passover feast the following Saturday. The festival of Passover recalls the dramatic confrontation between the power and authority of God on one hand and the stubborn will and hard heart of the Egyptian Pharaoh on the other. In the book of Exodus, God sent ten plagues to the Egyptians, the last of which caused the death of all firstborn sons. The Israelites were saved by placing the blood of the sacrificial lamb on their doorposts, thus causing death to "pass over" them. We learn of the courage and faithfulness of Moses as he led the Israelites out of the bonds of slavery and toward the path to freedom. Jewish people for over three thousand years have memorialized this important historical event with a prayer service and meal called the Passover Seder.

What are some of the elements of the Passover Seder? Let's describe the various components of this feast.

The Passover festivities begin in the dining room of someone's home. Following the lighting of candles and the ritual of hand washing, the head of the household reads the Passover narrative from the book of Exodus.

The meal begins with the removal of leavened bread from the room. In Jewish tradition, leavened bread signifies the potential for both corruption and sin. Removing the bread demonstrates a willingness to remove any corrupting influence in one's life and to submit to God in obedience. The Passover meal includes matzah, or unleavened bread, first baked in the harsh desert sun of the Middle East.

The centerpiece of the meal, of course, is a roasted lamb. The lamb symbolizes the Passover lamb that was sacrificed to God so that the Israelite infants might live. Traditionally, the blood of the lamb was placed in the doorposts of Jewish homes, marking them for salvation.

A sprig of celery or parsley is also served at the meal. This gift from the vegetable garden represents newness of life, which is created by God. It is a reminder that God is a faithful provider of sustenance to his people. The celery or parsley is dipped in salt water before it is eaten, calling to mind that life in Egypt was difficult and filled with pain, suffering, and tears.

Bitter herbs (horseradish is often used) are served on a piece of matzah. These bitter herbs symbolize the bitterness of slave life in Egypt.

There are four times during the meal when a sip of wine is taken. These four sips represent freedom, deliverance, redemption, and thanksgiving. The Passover meal is also filled with the singing of hymns, which precedes each of the four sips of wine.

The Jewish Passover feast just described is essential to understanding the events of our Christian Holy Week. In fact, the Orthodox Christian date for Pascha is determined by the date of celebration of the Jewish Passover. There is a vital link between the Passover of the Jews during the time of Moses and the sacrifice and victory of Christ during this new "Passover." How so?

- Jesus is the Lamb sacrificed on Golgotha. He shed his blood for us for the forgiveness of our sins and for life everlasting. Jesus is called the "Lamb of God" for a reason. Instead of many lambs being sacrificed for all the faithful, Jesus became the Lamb sacrificed once, for everyone, on Golgotha.

- In the sacrament of the Eucharist, Jesus instituted a new covenant with his people. The old covenant enabled only one priest, the high priest, to offer a sacrifice once a year on behalf of the people. Jesus allows us to enter into the symbolic "Holy Place" every time we receive the Eucharist. We affirm this new covenant each time we receive Holy Communion. Jesus instructs us at the Last Supper, "Do this in remembrance of me."

- Christ is the host of this new Passover Seder. He invites us to partake of this heavenly banquet.

- The Jewish Passover is preceded by the removal of leavened bread from the household. Christians are called to drive the leaven of sin from our lives if we are to partake of the Passover of Christ, the Eucharist.

- The Jewish Passover meal is to be shared by the whole family. The Christian Passover, the Eucharist, is to be shared by the family of faith, the body of Christ—the Church.

So as we approach the events of this Holy Week, be cognizant of the link between the Jewish Passover and the new Christian Passover. As we read the scriptural passages and sing the hymns of the coming week, seek Christ, the Passover Lamb, whose death on the cross saves humankind from sin and death.

In closing, these verses from the book of Exodus clearly link the Jewish Passover with the Christian Passover:

> This day shall be a day of remembrance for you. You shall celebrate it as a festival to the Lord; throughout your generations you shall observe it as a perpetual ordinance . . . And when your children ask you, "What do you mean by this observance?" you shall say, "It is the passover sacrifice to the Lord, for he passed over the houses of the Israelites in Egypt, when he struck down the Egyptians but spared our houses." And the people bowed down and worshipped. (Exod 12:14, 26–27)

JESUS IN GETHSEMANE

In the seventeenth chapter of the Gospel of John, Jesus reveals intimate facets of his prayer life. Having completed his volatile three-year ministry, Jesus prepares for his impending arrest, betrayal, Crucifixion, suffering, death—and his eventual Resurrection. His public ministry included many encounters and interactions with people of all stripes: the healing of a paralytic, the preaching to thousands in the temple and on hillsides, the debates with lawyers and scribes, the befriending of thieves and prostitutes, and the teaching of wisdom to his disciples and inner circle.

Yet Jesus finds himself in the Garden of Gethsemane seemingly alone. At this crucial juncture, he calls on the only One who could understand his predicament. In this chapter we learn some of the vital and life-giving components of prayer. In even his most desperate hour, Jesus models for us the path to truth, peace, and reassurance. Let us concentrate on four specific verses from this chapter that may help to expand our experience of prayer.

Jesus glorifies God the Father (v. 1). Often we are so consumed with our station in life that our first action in prayer is to blather on about our concerns and needs. Yet Jesus reminds us that the first words on our lips need to be ones of praise and glory for God. Awe and gratitude to our Creator should fit in right behind this praise and glory. First things first: let us lift up our eyes to the heavens with adoration.

Jesus states, "This is eternal life, that they may know you, the only true God, and Jesus Christ whom you have sent" (v. 3). This verse provides a definitive statement about who we are and what we are created for. We are called to be in communion with God in this life and to strive to be with God in eternal life. When we begin with this premise, all our subsequent priorities are refocused. Our problems and concerns seem less daunting, and we become less selfish. This verse is also instrumental in reminding us that prayer is not an exercise in trying to change God's mind, but instead involves asking God to redirect our lives toward his will. We say in the Lord's Prayer, "Thy will be done, on earth as it is in heaven."

Jesus states, "I glorified you on earth by finishing the work that you gave me to do" (v. 4). Jesus was given a job to do on earth. He took on flesh, he taught us about the love of God, he sacrificed his life on the cross, he rose from the dead, and now he offers us eternal life. We might say that Jesus successfully completed his tasks. Likewise, in our own prayer time we must continually seek God's guidance as to what our task(s) is (are) here on earth, what our work is that will glorify God. "How can I use my time, talents, and possessions to love God and serve others?" The answer to this question will change over the course of time. As we continue to evolve and mature, our ways of serving will progress as well.

Jesus states, "I pray for them" (v. 9 KJV). Jesus demonstrates the need for intercessory prayer. Besides making us less selfish, St. John of Kronstadt reminds us, "Prayer for others is beneficial to the man himself who prays; it purifies the heart, strengthens faith and hope in God, and arouses love for God and neighbor."[23] Intercessory prayer aims for the highest goals—unity, oneness, wholeness. Jesus's final desire in Gethsemane is to unite the body of believers with God.

Both clergy and laity are called to be intercessors. For example, the clergy extend intercessory prayers during the *Proskomide* service, which is offered just before the Divine Liturgy. While preparing the *prosphora* (bread with seal) for the Eucharist, the priest calls to mind the names of both the living and deceased for commemoration.

The laity can express their prayers of intercession in many ways. When reciting the Jesus Prayer, "Lord Jesus Christ, Son of God, have mercy on me," a lay person might include the name of someone in need: "Lord Jesus Christ, Son of God, have mercy on Mary." Whether praying for a loved one, an adversary, or for the resolution to a problem, the Jesus Prayer is an effective form of intercessory prayer.

In verse twenty of this chapter, Jesus implies that intercessory prayer extends to future generations when he prays for "those who *will* believe in me." Have you ever considered praying for the future of your parish or for the spouses of your young children and grandchildren? Jesus models for us that prayer is outside time and space. The saints and holy people of the past intercede for us, and we can intercede for the faithful in the future. Even in his most distressing moment, before his arrest and Crucifixion, Jesus models for us this truth: one God, one faith, and one body, now and forever.

MOTHER'S DAY

There is a humorous proverb that says: "God could not be everywhere, so he created mothers." A mother's job description is overwhelming. In addition to providing practical benefits to her children, such as food, clothing, and shelter, a mother also takes on the responsibility of shaping, molding, and guiding her children. Most importantly, a mother is entrusted with developing the spiritual life of her family. A child's first impression of God is often linked to his or her mother. This staggering list of maternal duties, however, must also be balanced with the amusing dimensions of motherhood.

Author Erma Bombeck writes a humorous story of how mothers were created. She writes that on that day God had already worked overtime:

An angel said to him, "Lord, you sure are spending a lot of time on this one." The Lord turned and said, "Have you read the specs on this model? She is supposed to be completely washable, but not plastic. She is to have 180 moving parts, all of them replaceable. She is to have a kiss that will heal everything from a broken leg to a broken heart. She is to have a lap that will disappear whenever she stands up. She is to be able to function on black coffee and leftovers. And she is supposed to have six pairs of hands."

"Six pairs of hands," said the angel, "that's impossible." "It's not the six pairs of hands that bother me," said the Lord, "It's the three pairs of eyes. She is supposed to have one pair that sees through closed doors so that whenever she says, 'What are you kids doing in there?' she already knows what they're doing in there. She has another pair in the back of her head to see all the things she is not supposed to see but must see. And then she has one pair right in front that can look at a child that just goofed and communicate love and understanding without saying a word."

"That's too much," said the angel, "You can't put that much in one model. Why don't you rest for awhile and resume your creating tomorrow?" "No, I can't," said the Lord, "I'm close to creating someone very much like myself. I've already come up with a model who can heal herself when she is sick—who can feed a family of six with one pound of hamburger—and who can persuade a nine-year-old to take a shower."

Then the angel looked at the model of motherhood a little more closely and said, "She's too soft." "Oh, but she is tough," said the Lord. "You'd be surprised how much this mother can do."

"Can she think?" asked the angel. "Not only can she think," said the Lord, "but she can reason, and compromise, and persuade."

Then the angel reached over and touched her cheek. "This one has a leak. I told you that you couldn't put that much in one model." "That's not a leak," said the Lord, "That's a tear."

"What's that for?" asked the angel. "Well it's for joy, for sadness, for sorrow, for disappointment, for pride." "You're a genius!" said the angel. And the Lord said, "Oh, but I didn't put the tear there."[24]

Mother's Day is special because we recognize that a mother's love is probably the closest example we have to God's love. It is a love that is life giving, unconditional, and eternal. A mother's love sacrifices for her own offspring, and this love even extends to other children in need. When I was a young boy, my own mother used to tell me that if I ever got lost or separated from her in a big crowd, I should look for a mother who was pushing a baby in a stroller or holding a young child by the hand and ask her to help me look for my mother. What is safer in such situations than appealing to a mother's love?

We often speak about God the Father in our faith, but there is an interesting image in Scripture that depicts God's love for us as a mother loving her own child. In Isaiah 49 we read the Israelites crying out to God, "The Lord has forsaken me, my Lord has forgotten me" (v. 14). God responds in this way: "Can a woman forget her nursing child, or show no compassion for the child of her womb? Even these may forget, yet I will not forget you. See, I have inscribed you on the palms of my hands" (vv. 15–16).

This passage reminds us of how a child is born and receives nourishment from his or her mother. But this passage speaks not only about the physical caring of a child, but of the emotional intensity that bonds a mother to her offspring. Biologically producing children does not make one a wonderful mother. Being a *true* mother is an act of the heart. In this Scripture passage, God tells his people how intensely he feels his love for them. He is saying to them, "I will sustain you. I will not forget you. I will nourish you even in your time of trial."

Isn't it amazing that whenever God describes the nature of his relationship with his people, he always speaks of it by comparing it to the most intense relationships human beings have with one another? God never compares our relationship with him to a business arrangement or a casual relationship, because he is not an impersonal life force. God is always described as our Father; or compared to a mother, as in the passage from Isaiah; or likened to a bridegroom, as in in Jesus's parable; or depicted as a friend who is closer than a brother and who lays down his life for us. That's how magnificent God's love is for each of us. That's also how special mothers should be to us. Happy Mother's Day!

MEMORIALS OF LIFE AND FAITH (MEMORIAL DAY)

Tomorrow our country celebrates Memorial Day. It is a time set aside to honor those men and women in the armed services who sacrificed their lives in defense of our nation. This holiday was instituted soon after the Civil War with the following declaration: "The 30th day of May, 1868, is designated for the purpose of strewing with flowers or otherwise decorating the graves of comrades who died in defense of their country during the late rebellion."[25] After World War I, the day was expanded to recognize and honor soldiers of all American wars. For us who are fortunate enough to live in the United States, Memorial Day is a time to remember the price that has been paid for our freedom. What is it about remembering that is so important to the human condition?

In Washington DC stands the Lincoln Memorial. Designed by Henry Bacon on a plan similar to the Parthenon in Greece, the structure includes thirty-six columns made of marble. These columns surround the building, each representing one of the United States (both on the Union and Confederate sides) that existed in Lincoln's time. Inside, there sits a colossal, nineteen-foot, seated statue of Lincoln. The statue dominates the interior and looks eastward across a reflecting pool with a view of the Washington Monument and the Capitol. On the south wall is inscribed Lincoln's Gettysburg Address, and on the north wall is his Second Inaugural Address. The cornerstone was laid in 1915, and it was completed and dedicated on Memorial Day in 1922. We have the Lincoln Memorial to help future generations remember Abraham Lincoln, and to remember the things that he accomplished in his lifetime. We might say that Memorial Day and the Lincoln Memorial are examples of how we keep significant people and events alive in our memory.

This act of creating memorials is not limited to our nation's history. Throughout the Old and New Testaments, memorials were established to help remind us of the power and presence of God. One Old Testament example that we can draw from is recorded in the book of Joshua. The Israelites had wandered in the desert for forty years, free from the Egyptians but still not having come into the land of Canaan, which

God had promised them. Joshua led the Israelites to the banks of the Jordan River; they were ready to cross over the water into the Promised Land. The Jordan, however, was overflowing and impossible to cross. God instructed Joshua to have the priests carry the Ark of the Covenant (which contained the tablets with the Ten Commandments) into the water. God promised that by doing so, the flowing waters would stop and the Israelites would be able to pass into the Promised Land. This happened exactly as God had foretold, and the joyful Israelites entered the blessings of Canaan.

But the narrative does not end there. After crossing, Joshua instructed twelve people, one from each tribe, to carry a large rock from the bottom of the Jordan River to the Canaanite side of the riverbank. Why did Joshua have these twelve stones purposely constructed after the miracle crossing? He tells us, "These stones shall be to the Israelites a memorial forever" (Josh 4:7). Joshua continues,

> When your children ask their parents in time to come, "What do these stones mean?" then you shall let your children know, "Israel crossed over the Jordan here on dry land." For the Lord your God dried up the waters of the Jordan for you until you crossed over. (4:21–23)

Joshua, through God's wisdom, understood the power of memorials for the human person.

For Orthodox Christians, there are many memorials we can use to support our faith: sites in the Holy Land, shrines of saints, relics of saints, and wonder-working icons, to name a few. But in the New Testament there is one unique memorial that has a great impact on our spiritual lives, and in which we participate at each Divine Liturgy—the Eucharist. During the Last Supper, Jesus took bread and wine and instructed his disciples to eat and drink of these new memorials. In the Liturgy of St. Basil, the priest recites, "Do this in remembrance of me; for as often as you eat this bread and drink this cup, you proclaim my death and resurrection."

The Eucharist, the living presence of Jesus Christ, is a memorial established for our growth, healing, forgiveness, strength, and reassurance. But this memorial does more than simply help us recognize a past event or person. The key to understanding this memorial is found in the Greek word for "memorial" or "memory": *anamnisi*. The Greek term implies reliving or reexperiencing, in this case the Last Supper, as if we were present at the original event. As an *anamnisi*, the Eucharist is real and alive in the present, and is not just an historical event. The Eucharistic memorial, established by Christ, has sustained Christians for centuries and will nurture the faithful until his glorious Second Coming. As St. John of Kronstadt tells us,

> What is there to be wondered at in the Lord's offering you his Body and Blood as food and drink? He who has given you as food the flesh of the animals he created has finally given you himself as food and drink . . . that you should become an inheritor of the kingdom of heaven, for which reason you were created, and for which you live.[26]

Sermons for Summer

Childlike vs. Childish

In the Gospel of St. Luke, Christ tells us to be like children. We read:

Let the little children come to me, and do not stop them; for it is to such as these that the kingdom of God belongs. Truly I tell you, whoever does not receive the kingdom of God as a little child will never enter it. (18:16–17)

What is it about children that Jesus wants us to emulate? Before we investigate this question too seriously, I want to recommend a little book entitled *Children's Letters to God*,[27] which is a compilation of brief letters written by children to God. Listen to some of these gems in order to put us in the right spirit for our topic:

Dear God:
    Thank you for the baby brother, but what I really wanted was a puppy.

Dear God:
    My grandpa says you were around when he was a little boy. How far back do you go?

Dear God:

I bet it is very hard for you to love everybody in the whole world. There are only four people in our family and I can never do it.

We must make a distinction between the terms *childlike* and *childish*. Those of you who have children or grandchildren know that childish behavior includes conduct that is self-centered and disobedient. Childlike qualities, on the other hand, reveal basic Christian characteristics. For example:

Children recognize their dependence on others and look for help from others as a matter of course.

Children are not impressed with rank or title. They tend to be less prejudiced than adults.

Children are honest with their feelings. They hold nothing back when expressing themselves to others.

Children are inquisitive. They are sponge-like, constantly learning and growing and getting excited about new experiences.

Children find it easier to trust others more than adults do. Place a child on a table and tell that child to jump in your arms, and he or she will do it without hesitation—such is a child's trust.

Children are naturally joyful and playful. My daughter races to the window with excitement whenever she sees a bird outside, as if she is seeing one for the first time.

Children bear no grudges. They are uninhibited, eager to please, pure of heart, and have numerous other laudable qualities that we could list.

Although we can never be children again, Jesus calls us to cultivate childlike qualities in our relationship with God. Think for a moment about how you relate with God. As you reflect on your connection with God, ask yourself: in what ways are you still trusting, honest with your feelings, inquisitive, joyful, and pure of heart?

There are two other letters in this book that offer us great insight into how adults can rekindle the gift of being childlike in our relationship with God. The first letter states:

Dear God:

I think about you sometimes even when I'm not praying.

The second follows:

Dear God:

I don't ever feel alone since I found out about you.

Both of these brief yet profound letters underscore that true faith is about a personal and daily relationship with God. These two children experience the presence of God as a natural part of their lives. Sometimes as adults we overintellectualize our faith. Children, on the other hand, have the ability to perceive without understanding, to feel without analyzing.

During the Divine Liturgy we are exhorted to "taste and see how good is the Lord." We are being invited to first *experience* the Lord so that we may then come to *understand* him also.

It is ironic that adults are expected to be role models for children. The reality is that adults have quite a lot to learn from children. May we imitate their enthusiasm so that each of us may breathe a true faith that is centered on a personal and daily relationship with God.

THE BEHEADING OF JOHN THE BAPTIST

Today we honor the memory and ministry of St. John the Baptist. The more notable celebration of John takes place on January 7, but today we pause to reflect on his martyrdom. John is considered the last prophet of the Old Testament. Prophets before him, such as Jeremiah, Isaiah, and Elijah, attempted to bring the Israelites back to their spiritual roots. Most times, these messengers of God were rejected by the Jewish faithful, with John being no exception.

The contemporary Christian might think it difficult to relate to prophets in general, and John in particular. Yet we share many personality traits with this man whom we consider the forerunner of our Lord and Savior Jesus Christ. Several Gospel passages highlight the wide array of human qualities that make John a fascinating subject of study.

We first meet the adult John in the desert as a charismatic preacher and ascetic. His zealousness and strong convictions brought many out to the desert to hear his message of repentance. John despised the hypocrisy of the Pharisees and Sadducees, and fearlessly sought truth and justice. His preaching included an invitation to be baptized with water, a ritual cleansing common during that time. The personality trait exhibited by John during this period of his life might be termed **boldness**.

We next witness John fulfilling his role as prophet. While ministering to his followers, John recognizes Jesus as the expected messiah and proclaims, "Here is the Lamb of God!" (John 1:29). John initially rejects Jesus's request that John baptize him, saying, "I need to be baptized by you, and do you come to me?" (Matt 3:14). John relents, being obedient to Jesus's appeal for baptism. Acknowledging the greatness of Jesus, John makes clear his role as forerunner to Christ by stating, "He must increase, but I must decrease" (John 3:30). This second personality trait that John displayed is **humility**.

The third attribute that John demonstrates surfaces in an equally public forum. He expresses outrage at the adulterous relationship between Herod, ruler of Galilee, and Herodias, his brother Philip's wife. John bravely challenges the establishment at great personal risk. He is eventually imprisoned by an enraged and embarrassed Herod, who chains John in a barbaric chamber for prisoners. This third personality trait that resonates with the modern Christian is composed of both **courage** and **moral outrage**.

The fourth expression of John's personality is one that is common to the human condition. While in prison, we see another facet of John, albeit an unexpected one—he expresses doubt. John sends some of his disciples to question Jesus, "Are you the one who is to come, or are we to wait for another?" (Matt 11:4). Jesus responds gently, "Go and tell John what you hear and see: the blind receive their sight, the lame walk, the lepers are cleansed, the deaf hear, the dead are raised, and the poor have good news brought to them" (Matt 11:4–5). Though bold and courageous and fearless, John experiences a hint of **doubt**.

The fifth personality trait that characterizes the beloved John relates to his martyrdom. Herod is celebrating a birthday with many eminent guests in attendance. The daughter of Herodias offers a provocative dance as a gift to Herod. Enticed by this expression, Herod promises to grant anything to the young woman. Prompted by her mother, she requests the head of John the Baptist on a platter. Though Herod respected John, viewing him as a prophet, he commanded the prison guards to have John beheaded, in order to fulfill his oath. Therefore, the final characteristic that John demonstrates to the Christian faithful is **willing obedience**.

Jesus articulates the highest compliment about John the Baptist, recorded in the Gospel of Matthew: "Truly I tell you, among those born of women no one has arisen greater than John the Baptist" (Matt 11:11). He models for us so many of the best human qualities. Throughout our lives we, too, can demonstrate the full spectrum of emotions, paralleling John in expressing boldness, humility, courage, moral outrage, doubt, and willing obedience.

The challenge for the contemporary Christian is to refine these personality traits, directing them for the glory of God. The goal for the practicing Christian is not to deaden the expression of our unique qualities, but rather to purify them in ways that imitate Christ and the saints. By doing so we will be following the holy example of St. John the Baptist:

> See, I am sending my messenger to prepare the way before me,
> and the Lord whom you seek will suddenly come to his temple.
> The messenger of the covenant in whom you delight—indeed,
> he is coming, says the Lord of hosts. But who can endure the
> day of his coming, and who can stand when he appears? For he
> is like a refiner's fire and like fullers' soap; he will sit as a refiner

and purifier of silver, and he will purify the descendants of Levi and refine them like gold and silver, until they present offerings to the Lord in righteousness. (Mal 3:1–3)

AN OVERVIEW OF CHURCH HISTORY[28]

33 AD	Pentecost
33–313	Persecution of Christians (all apostles martyred except John)
ca. 36	Conversion of Paul, the great missionary and writer of fourteen New Testament Epistles
ca. 70–100	The document *The Teaching of the Twelve Apostles* (*Didache*) outlines the basic structure of the Divine Liturgy
ca. 50–100	Writing of New Testament Gospels and Epistles
ca. 150	St. Justin Martyr describes the liturgical worship of the Church, centered on the Eucharist
312	Conversion of Emperor Constantine to Christianity
325	First Ecumenical Council takes place in Nicea. In all, seven ecumenical councils take place between the fourth and eighth centuries
3rd–early 4th c.	Monasticism begins to flourish, initially led by Sts. Anthony and Pachomius; Desert Fathers and Mothers flee mainstream Church for the desert
367	St. Athanasius writes letter first establishing (or acknowledging) canon of New Testament; Church council in Hippo in 393 affirms canon
988	Conversion of Russia, followed by great missionary activity
1054	Schism between Eastern (Orthodox) and Western (Roman Catholic) Church

12th–13th c.   Crusades by Western Church further scar relations
                     between Roman Catholic and Orthodox Churches;
                     specifically the Fourth Crusade (1202–4)

1453   Ottoman Empire overruns Constantinople;
                     Byzantine Empire ends, forcing many Orthodox to
                     live in a persecuted state

1517   Martin Luther posts Ninety-Five Theses, beginning
                     the Protestant Reformation against the Roman
                     Catholic Church

1794   Missionaries arrive in Alaska; Orthodoxy
                     introduced to North America by Sts. Herman and
                     Innocent

20th c.   Communist (atheistic) rule dominates traditional
                     Orthodox countries in Russia and Eastern Europe

1890s–1924   Immigrants from traditional Orthodox countries
                     begin to arrive in America and establish parishes
                     based on ethnic backgrounds

ORTHODOXY AND EVOLUTION

Does the name Chet Raymo mean anything to you? Dr. Raymo is a professor of physics at Stonehill College who writes a weekly science column for the *Boston Globe*. I've been reading his column for years, primarily because I find it fascinating how he addresses the topic of evolution on a regular basis.

Dr. Raymo is a strong advocate of the Big Bang theory, and he often chides those who adhere to the Judeo-Christian understanding of creation. My focus is not to undermine Dr. Raymo or science in general, because the Orthodox Church has historically held great respect for the sciences. Rather, I want to share with you a column that Dr. Raymo wrote recently, which offers an interesting perspective on the evolutionism/creationism debate.[29] The author uses a dialogue format, in this case a conversation between a professor and a doubting student. Listen to some excerpts of this exchange:

"Professor, that stuff you spoke of in class this morning—about the beginning of the universe . . ."

Yes?

"Well, you know how you said that the universe began 10 or 15 billion years ago as an infinitely small point . . .?"

Yes, that would appear to be the case. An explosion from a point of infinite energy. Space and time expanding from nothing. Matter coalescing from cooling radiation. Stars, galaxies . . .

"To tell you the truth, I'm having a hard time believing it. I mean, the idea that everything exists today, the billions of galaxies, stars, planets, life, everything, was contained within something no bigger than a pinprick. I mean, come on . . . Do you really expect me to swallow that?"

It's difficult to imagine, I'll grant you. But not impossible . . . the "impossible" can turn out to be true.

"But the whole universe contained within a pinprick?"

I'm not telling you to believe the Big Bang if you don't want to, but keep your options open.

"You're asking me to take it on faith."

Yes, on faith. But not blind faith. And besides, it's a wonderful story—a universe unfolding from a mathematical point!

"Yes, it's a wonderful story, alright, but . . ."

But what?

"But I still don't believe it."

For me this column was food for thought. And it challenged me to research the Orthodox understanding of evolution.

By definition, evolution is the change that the creative order has undergone over the course of generations. Evolutionists also espouse that all living organisms have descended from a common ancestor, and that new species have developed over time. Scientists claim that evolution is a fact, because it has been overwhelmingly validated by the evidence. For example, scientists have traced the development of the horse from an early dog-sized creature to the contemporary, larger animal. An Orthodox Christian would agree that creation has undergone changes over the course of history, affirming that evolution is a fact.

Yet even renowned paleontologist Steven Jay Gould acknowledges that evolution is also a theory:

Evolution is a theory. It is also a fact. And facts and theories are different things, not rungs in a hierarchy of increasing certainty. Facts are the world's data. Theories are structures of ideas that explain and interpret facts.[30]

In fact, there are many theories of evolution. One theory holds that the human person evolved from lower forms of life—from an ape or other such animal. Another theory holds that humankind's development was an accident, occurring by happenstance, independent of any cause or purpose. Many other theories of evolution circulate and continue to be developed.

What an informed Orthodox Christian must be aware of is that not all theories of evolution are compatible with our faith. The Orthodox Church does not view the Old Testament account of creation in a literal way—the Bible is not a science book—and so it is necessary to recognize the creative power of God in the process of evolution. Those theories that suggest a purely mechanistic understanding of evolution, without a place for God, are not compatible with the Orthodox view of creation.

Some might think, "So what? Should we care if God created the world or if we evolved from a chimpanzee? What connection does evolution have with my daily life or with my relationship with God?" I submit to you that there is a direct correlation between the evolutionary debate and our daily life. Our Christian faith is not only concerned with how we are created, but more importantly, with why we are created. Our faith teaches that we are created to be in fellowship with God. The human person is created in the image of God, which implies that we are of great value to God. Our integrity, our self-worth, and our meaning in life come from God, who loves us more than we know how to love. This respect and honor for every human being is visibly expressed in our worship when the priest censes not only the icons, but the members of the congregation, saluting the image of God in each person. These verses from Psalm 8 illustrate this point:

> O Lord, our Sovereign, how majestic is your name in all the earth! . . . When I look at your heavens, the work of your fingers, the moon and the stars that you have established; what are human beings that you are mindful of them, mortals that you care for them? Yet you have . . . crowned them with glory and honor. (vv. 1, 3–5)

The author never thinks of himself as a chance creation, a cosmic accident. God watches each of us tenderly, as a parent watches over his or her child. The psalmist is the object of God's knowledge and care.

There is a further point that demands our attention. Scripture teaches that in the beginning God created. What is most amazing for us today is that God is still creating. Every new tulip, every new blue jay, every new baby in the crib reveals God's creative energy. And yet God is still creating us; we are not finished products. These Scripture verses remind us that we continue to evolve, develop, and mature:

> Create in me a clean heart, O God, and put a new and right spirit within me . . . Restore to me the joy of your salvation, and sustain in me a willing spirit. (Ps 51:10, 12)

When you send forth your spirit, they [your creatures] are created; and you renew the face of the ground. (Ps 104:30)

To the doubting student in Dr. Raymo's article, the Church would respond by saying that evolution is a fact. But, by whatever method of creation—and there are many theories—God remains the Creator, without whom life is impossible.

THE UNFORGIVING SERVANT

In the Gospel passage often given the heading "The Parable of the Unforgiving Servant" (Matthew 18:23–35), Jesus tells the story of a servant who owed a tremendous debt, the equivalent of approximately one million dollars, and who pleaded for mercy from the king to whom he owed the money. After being forgiven this tremendous debt, this same servant came across a fellow servant who owed him just a few dollars, threatened him, and demanded payment from him.

The parable is an eloquent example of the tendency we have to plead for forgiveness from others and then to deny it to someone else when the roles are reversed. The author C. S. Lewis once noted, "Everyone says forgiveness is a lovely idea, until they have something to forgive."[31]

The theme of forgiveness is one of ultimate importance in the Christian life. Jesus not only modeled what it meant to be a forgiving person, he continually taught, especially through parables, the necessity of forgiveness. In fact, two of the last statements uttered by Christ while he was being crucified were related to forgiveness. One of these statements was Jesus's plea for the forgiveness of those who crucified him: "Father, forgive them; for they do not know what they are doing" (Luke 23:34). Soon after, Jesus forgave the repentant thief who was crucified with him (23:43).

So how can we, in imitation of Christ, learn to be more forgiving people? Let us consider one facet of this theme: the misconceptions that we have about the process of forgiveness. These misconceptions sometimes block our ability to forgive.

For example, one misconception we often have is that forgiving someone else lifts a burden from that person. The opposite is true. The person offering forgiveness experiences a sense of relief that allows him or her to move on. Corrie ten Boom, the famous Dutch survivor of a Nazi concentration camp during World War II, once commented,

> Those who were able to forgive their former enemies were able to return to the outside world and rebuild their lives, no matter what the physical scars. Those who nursed their bitterness remained invalids. It was as simple and as horrible as that.[32]

A second misconception about forgiveness we often have is that our hurt feelings immediately dissipate when we extend forgiveness to another person. The reality is that forgiveness is not an instantaneous, magical process. The movement from anger and hurt feelings to less intense emotions is a slow one, and the process of healing in general is sometimes extremely slow. Long after one has forgiven oneself and others, traces of different emotions may resurface at a later time. Metropolitan Anthony Bloom offers insight on this misconception:

> We must never confuse forgiving with forgetting, or imagine that these two things go together. Not only do they not belong together, but they are mutually exclusive . . . the only thing that must go, be erased from the past, is its venom; the bitterness, the resentment, the estrangement; but not the memory.[33]

A third misconception is that forgiveness means reconciliation. This notion implies that if we forgive someone, we ought to like that person. In fact, it is often true that we may dislike another person very much while we are actually in the process of forgiving him or her. Many saints of the Church point out that the first step toward forgiveness may be simply to not seek revenge or retribution. Evagrius, one of the Desert Fathers, has written: "It is not possible to love all the brethren to the same degree. But it is possible to associate with all in a manner that is . . . free of resentment and hatred."[34]

Evagrius also points out that the ability to forgive is not based on feelings but on a decision: either to hold onto those hurt feelings, or to forgive. Both choices have their own implications. The choice to forgive brings with it a sense of relief and a feeling of a burden lifted. We forgive not because that is what good people do, but because it is what we need for our own wholeness and for the well-being of those around us.

Anyone who has really struggled a long time to forgive knows that forgiveness is not a simple matter of willpower. The beginning of forgiveness may take months or possibly years of asking God for help to even want to forgive. In fact, we may only be able to forgive when we allow God's presence to seep into our injured and painful souls.

In your next quiet time with God, consider entering a dialogue with God on the following reflection:

> Lord, who are the people I must decide to forgive? Is it a family member, a friend, a co-worker? Do I need to forgive myself?

Lord, I know that forgiveness is a prerequisite for becoming a life-filled and life-giving person. Let your forgiving love flow through my heart to heal all discord, restore harmony, and renew a loving spirit within me.

ST. NICODEMUS OF THE HOLY MOUNTAIN
ON SPIRITUAL WARFARE[35]

The arena, the field of battle, the site where the fight actually
takes place is in our own heart. The time of battle is our whole
life.[36]

These words of wisdom were written by St. Nicodemus of
the Holy Mountain, whose memory we commemorate on
July 14. St. Nicodemus was one of the most prolific and eminent writers
of the eighteenth century. He was at once a hymnographer, hagiographer,
canonist, liturgist, ascetic, and biblical commentator. But it is his spiritual works that have been of most influence.

The theme of one book that he edited, *Unseen Warfare*, is the inner
struggle that every Christian undertakes from the moment of baptism.
The reader of this spiritual classic learns wise counsel on how to conquer
the invisible foes in order to acquire the divine treasure, which is union
with God both in this life and in the kingdom of heaven.

Let us briefly reflect on several quotations from *Unseen Warfare* in
order to gain a deeper understanding of St. Nicodemus and his message:

Examine your actions with the utmost strictness and explore
deeply into their causes. The more deeply you explore into all
that happens in you and comes from you, eliminating all wrong
things and affirming right things, the more quickly you will
cleanse your conscience; just as the deeper the well, the purer
the water.[37]

You must know that the progress on the path of spiritual life
differs greatly from an ordinary journey. If a traveler stops on his
ordinary journey, he loses nothing of the way already covered.
But if a traveler on the path of virtue stops in his spiritual progress, he loses much of the virtues previously acquired.[38]

Take up arms against the passion which troubles you most. Fight
it with your whole strength and strive to establish yourself in the
virtue opposed to that passion. For as soon as you succeed in
this, you will bring to life all other virtues in yourself.[39]

When you read the scriptures do not have in mind to read page after page, but ponder over each word. When some words make you go deep into yourself, or stir you to contrition, or fill your heart with spiritual joy and love, pause on them. It means that God draws near to you.[40]

If you wish your prayer to bring much fruit, never be content by oral prayer alone, but pray also with your mind and heart—using your mind to understand and be conscious of all that is said in words, and your heart to feel it all. Above all, pray with your heart. Prayer bursting from the heart is like a streak of lightning, which takes but a moment to cross the heavens and appear before the throne of the all-merciful God.[41]

Every time you fall into some transgression, even if it happens a thousand times a day, as soon as you notice it, do not torture yourself and so waste your time without profit, but at once humble yourself, and, conscious of your weakness, turn to God with hope and call to Him from the depths of your heart.[42]

Whatever work you may undertake, however glorious, and with whatever effort and sacrifice you may accomplish it, it will not lead you to your desired spiritual aim if you leave your passions without attention, giving them freedom to live and act in you.[43]

Each morning try to examine and foresee all the situations you are likely to face in the course of the day which may give a chance to do one or another good action, and accompany this with a firm desire and resolve to make use of them without fail. In the evening examine yourself as to whether your good thoughts and desires of the morning were put into practice and how they were fulfilled.[44]

What are some of the lessons to be drawn from the writings of St. Nicodemus? What first stands out is the practical nature of his counsel. His advice is not limited to monastics; rather, it also applies to Christians living in the world. He seeks to integrate faith and life, without becoming weighed down in abstract nuances.

What also is modeled for contemporary audiences is St. Nicodemus's humility in portraying himself as a student of the faith, not as an authoritarian expert. He shares his own experiences of unseen warfare but without appearing condescending to the reader. The saint's unassuming nature, however, should not belie the fact that he exhibited immense knowledge of Holy Scripture and the writings of Church Fathers. He could recite long passages of holy writings from memory, immersing himself in the spiritual tools of the faith. St. Nicodemus remains an illuminating figure in the Church, combining intelligence, humility, and a pragmatic approach to the development of our souls.

THE PARAKLESIS SERVICE

One of the beautiful characteristics of the Orthodox faith is the liturgical cycle of services. Worship in the Church is a rhythmic pattern of fast periods leading to a feast. The liturgical cycle allows time for preparation, reflection, and then . . . celebration!

On August 15 Orthodox Christians celebrate the Dormition, or Falling Asleep, of the Theotokos. This feast honors the Virgin Mary, through whom the mystery of the Incarnation took place. The two weeks preceding the feast, August 1–14, are a time of prayer and fasting. During this period the Church offers a wonderful prayer service called the "Paraklesis to the Theotokos."

For anyone who suffers from grief, depression, sorrow, or anxiety, the Paraklesis is a welcome salve on the soul. Although the gospel message of Jesus Christ is one of joy, the Paraklesis service recognizes that everyone, from time to time, experiences emotional and spiritual pain. Rather than isolating ourselves or feeling shame over our distress, the Paraklesis extends to us an invitation to share that pain with the Theotokos, asking for her prayers and comfort.

Listen to these verses from hymns chanted during the service:

I entreat you, O Virgin,
Disperse the storm of my grief,
And the soul's most inward confusion,
Scatter it far from me.[45]

Heal me from the ills,
O Most Pure One, which the passions bring,
Make me worthy of your guiding care,
And unto me grant health,
Through your intercessions and your prayers.[46]

Whatever emotional or spiritual state we find ourselves in, the message throughout the Paraklesis service is that God accepts and affirms us. We are welcomed and consoled whether our suffering is from despair or hopelessness, fear or isolation, grief or rejection. It is important to note that not once does the Paraklesis attribute our suffering to a lack of faith. Instead, we are allowed to see things as they are and to give voice to our feelings. Being permitted to say things as they are, without being forced to say them as they "should" be or "must" be, can be cathartic and transformative.

The Paraklesis service, however, does not leave us in our wounded state. We are invited to start where we are emotionally and spiritually, and to slowly ascend to enlightenment, peace, hope, and the knowledge that God is the Physician of our souls and bodies. Below are several verses from the service that illustrate this point:

> Pure one, fill my heart
> With a merriment, a happiness;
> Bestow on me your spotless joy.[47]

> Dissipate the cloud
> Of my sinfulness, O bride of God,
> With the brightness of your eminence;
> For you brought forth the Light
> The Divine, which was before all time.[48]

We seek to pass through our sorrows, not to revel in them. As much as we cannot avoid the experience of darkness, so too we can never become so accustomed to dwelling therein that we do not try to find the light. This service is a holy avenue toward that light.

So how can one benefit liturgically from the Dormition fast?

1. Attend as many of the Paraklesis services as you can. Offered on most weeknights, the service is completed in less than one hour. By following along in the service book or chanting together with the congregation, you can find hope and inner peace from the Paraklesis on a daily basis. Many find the melodies so uplifting and infectious that they begin chanting portions of the service at home during their own prayer time.

2. Write a list of names of those whom you would like to intercede for and submit it to your parish priest. The Paraklesis service not only seeks the intercessions of the Theotokos for ourselves, but also calls us to intercede for others. Writing the names of friends and foes on a prayer list is a concrete expression of our love for others.

3. Write a list of concerns and pray about them during the service. Jesus wants us to share with him all of our thoughts, desires, and challenges in life. Writing a list of concerns and lifting them up

to God is a sign of trust and openness. It welcomes God into the most intimate places of our soul.

By God's grace, may we enter this Dormition fast period with a sense of purpose and expectation, crying out to the Mother of God:

> For those
> In great sorrow you are joy,
> And for the oppressed, a protection,
> And for the hungry, their food,
> Comfort unto those estranged;
> You are a staff to the blind,
> Visitation of all those sick,
> And to those held by pain
> Shelter and a comforting,
> And to the orphaned, an aid;
> Mother of our God in the highest,
> You who are the Spotless One, hasten,
> Save your servants from their sin, we ask of you.[49]

ARE WE PREPARED FOR DEATH?

everal years ago a lecture was offered by Bishop Kallistos
Ware (now Metropolitan Kallistos), a well-known speaker
and author. Though the topic was missions, the most memorable part
of the day was a question-and-answer session following the presentation.
A person from the audience raised a hand and inquired, "What is the
meaning of life?" A murmur in the crowd followed the question, many
wondering, "How can the bishop address such an open-ended and philosophical question in the limited time available?"

Without missing a beat, the bishop responded, "Your question is
indeed an interesting one. But to truly answer it we must first consider
another question: what is the meaning of *death*? When we have first an-
swered this question, then we will be able to respond to the issue of the
meaning of life."

The purpose of this reflection is not to offer a definitive treatise on
death, but to gently raise our awareness of the impending reality of our
own death. This does not have to be a morbid or undesirable topic to
ponder. As Christians, we should feel encouraged to contemplate any
subject with openness and trust. Perhaps the first place to begin a dialogue on death is to study the Church's teaching on the subject. The
Church teaches that, in principle, we should not die, because we were
created for life, not death. In the book of Genesis, we read that death was
not God's original plan for us. Yet humanity, as a creation of God, was
dependent upon communion with God in love and obedience. With the
appearance of sin, death entered into the equation.

This is the theological understanding of death—the "by-the-book"
answer, if you will. But what are our thoughts and feelings concerning
death, especially our own death? Is death something so terrible that we
are better off not thinking or talking about it? Or, is it possible to come
to terms with our dying, trusting that we have nothing to fear? Is it possible to prepare for our death with the same attentiveness that our parents
had in preparing for our birth? Death is the most universal human event,
something we all must contemplate. Yet how does our view of death color
our every day lives?

Perhaps one way to reflect on the passage from life to death is for each of us to consider the deaths of loved ones and their effects on us over time. I often reflect on my grandmother, who passed away many years ago. Her death has been a great loss—but also a great gift. A loss because so many people, including myself, can no longer visit with her and find new hope just by being in her presence. During difficult times in my life, when I experienced anguish and despair, she was always available. Many times she would pull my head to her chest and pray for me without words but with a spirit-filled silence that made me rise up from her embrace with new vitality.

Yet her death has been a gift as well. The beauty of a holy life is that it bears fruit long after its presence in this world comes to an end. Jesus states, "Very truly, I tell you, unless a grain of wheat falls into the earth and dies, it remains just a single grain; but if it dies, it bears much fruit" (John 12:24). Years after my grandmother's death, she continues to bear fruit in my life. I am deeply aware that many of my major decisions since her death have been guided by her intercessions and inspiration.

This is the mystery of Jesus's death and of the deaths of all who have lived a faithful life in Christ. Their lives yield fruit far beyond the limits of their short existence on earth. This is the hope-giving beauty of death. Death may be the end of our success, our productivity, or our fame. But it is not the end of our fruitfulness. Rather, the exquisiteness of life is that it can bear fruit long after life on earth has come to an end.

Thus the real question before us is not, "How much can I still accomplish?" or "How much influence can I still exert?" Instead, the true search for wisdom should include, "How can I live so that I can continue to bear fruit when I am no longer among family and friends?" If the Holy Spirit guides our lives—the Spirit of "love, joy, peace, patience, kindness, generosity, faithfulness, gentleness, and self-control" (Gal 5:22)—then that Spirit will not die, but will continue to grow from generation to generation.

THE GOOD SAMARITAN (ON COMPASSION)

I n Webster's Dictionary, the word *compassion* is defined as "the deep awareness of the suffering of another coupled with the wish to relieve it." Today's Gospel reading of the good Samaritan (Luke 10:25–37) illustrates compassion in action. The parable is well known to us all.

A man is robbed and left for dead by the side of the road. Two people, a priest and a Levite—people who should have known better—passed by the man in need. When the Samaritan, a hated person in Jewish society, sees the suffering victim, he stops and helps. He carries him on his animal to a nearby inn and even pays for his stay. Jesus concludes the parable by reminding his listeners to "go and do likewise" (v. 37).

The dictionary definition that I offered earlier seems to imply two parts to the meaning of compassion. First is realizing or being aware of the suffering of another, and second is acting on the desire to relieve that suffering. To rephrase that in Christian terms, compassion means being motivated by a love for Christ and then wanting to share that love with another person.

There is a story of a monk who lived alone in a cave in the Egyptian desert near the end of World War I. In the caves there were others also, but these were not monks. Rather, they were outcasts of society—lepers who had been abandoned by the nomadic tribes of the region. At the same time, a young British officer had become separated from his regiment in the midst of the fighting. After wandering in the desert for many days, he came across the monk's cave. The officer was half dead, and the old monk took him in and cared for him, slowly nursing him back to health. The old monk never said a word, but each day he would take food and water and disappear into the desert for several hours.

One day the officer offered to go with the monk, who nodded his assent. After a time they came upon a large cave. They entered, and when the officer's eyes adjusted to the light, he was aghast to see the people who inhabited this place. The old monk gently embraced each person, changing putrid bandages and cleaning oozing flesh. The officer was amazed at the old man's compassion and tenderness. All of this finally got to be too much for the officer, and he blurted out, "I would not do that for a million dollars." The monk turned to him and replied, "Neither would I." You see, for a million dollars the monk would not touch those running sores, but because Christ dwelt in his heart, he was moved with compassion to serve and love those outcasts.

A vital lesson of the Parable of the Good Samaritan is that compassion leads to healing. The monk brought hope and care to people who were rejected by society. As Christians, when we extend ourselves to those in pain, we become agents of healing. Although it is true that a person can be compassionate and not be Christian, a Christian cannot be fully a Christian without being compassionate.

Perhaps the story of the monk is too far-fetched or irrelevant for you. Allow me to share another story of compassion and healing, a true story that occurred in my former community.

There was a young woman who we will call "Sylvia." Like many young people, Sylvia was beguiled by the world. She graduated from college, enjoyed a good job, and was very popular. She had a bright future ahead of her. One day, however, Sylvia became sick. At first she thought she had the flu, but she continued to show symptoms over several weeks. After many rounds of tests, she was diagnosed with a rare form of connective tissue disease, which she was told would eventually cause total paralysis and death.

Sylvia was devastated. At first she refused to acknowledge the inevitable consequences of her illness. She became more intense in her worldly pursuits, until she began to lose control of her legs. Soon she was completely bedridden, unable to move. The several times I visited her she was angry and depressed. She wanted nothing to do with God or the Church. Despite Sylvia's strong feelings, her fellow parishioners reached out with care and compassion. People prepared meals for her; children sent her get-well cards; others cut her grass. After several months, and hours of talking, Sylvia began to accept her condition and even prepared for her death. She was so moved by the outpouring of compassion by the parish, she wanted to do something in return. But what could she do? At this point she was totally incapacitated. She began to pray for others. She prayed for the sick, for schoolchildren, and for our civil leaders. People started sending her prayer requests so that she could intercede on their behalf. Sylvia prayed many hours a day.

And do you know what? Sylvia became filled with love, totally reconciled with God, and exuded a peacefulness she had never known before.

This went on for two years, and before Sylvia died, she said that she had never been happier in her life. Even those around her experienced a tremendous spiritual rebirth and renewal in their faith.

The Parable of the Good Samaritan, the monk in the desert, and the example of Sylvia all point to the same truth: compassion leads to healing. When we become aware of someone's suffering and act on it, we release a power that in time proves irresistible. Compassion leads to healing; compassion leads to revitalized faith; compassion leads to the kingdom of heaven.

THE GAME OF LIFE[50]

I have been an avid chess player throughout my life. In my youth, I often participated in chess tournaments in New York, where the game enjoys great popularity. Although some might view chess as a frivolous game, I believe that many of the disciplines and guidelines needed to master chess are also applicable to experiencing the mystery of Christianity.

1. Know the Rules

Chess: You have to be educated to know how the pieces move; you must know how to play before you can win.

Christianity: An informed believer must know the basic tenets of the faith. For example, the goal of the Christian life is not simply to become moral, socially well-adjusted humans, but to develop and grow in our relationship with Jesus Christ and his Church.

2. Protect What Is Most Important

Chess: Protecting the king is the name of the game; the king's safety is paramount to winning the match.

Christianity: Protect your soul—you can accomplish much in life, but without protecting your soul all is lost.

3. Strategy/Planning

Chess: Very little can be accomplished without an overall plan and numerous related steps to accomplish the goal of winning the game.

Christianity: Scriptural examples of planning and preparing for the goal of salvation and union with God are numerous. Christ said that the builder must first consider the cost before beginning to build (Luke 14:28–30), and God told Jeremiah, "For surely I know the plans I have for you . . . plans for your welfare and not for harm, to give you a future with hope" (Jer 29:11).

4. Teamwork/Cooperation

Chess: Chess is a game that requires cooperation, teamwork, and the development of the game pieces for success.

Christianity: Christians are connected to something larger than themselves—they are members of the body of Christ. In St. Paul's writings, especially 1 Corinthians 10, he emphasizes the variety of gifts we each possess and the fact that we must work together, as cooperating members of a body. (Also see Acts 15 on the cooperation and teamwork of the apostles.)

5. Attentiveness/Discernment/Vigilance
Chess: Pay attention to little details; missing one can have catastrophic repercussions.
Christianity: The Greek word for "discern," *diakrino*, means to distinguish, or to separate out as to examine or scrutinize—see, for example, 1 Corinthians 11:29, which deals with discerning the Lord's Supper. Many spiritual writings of the Orthodox Church focus on the themes of vigilance and watchfulness as a means of protecting our souls.

6. Keep Thoughts Clear: Concentrate
Chess: A champion player will not be easily distracted by internal or external stimuli.
Christianity: In Orthodox spirituality, the terms *"nous"* and *"logismoi"* are essential in understanding the human person. Although difficult to translate, the *nous* is the eye of the soul, a spiritual vision that allows one to recognize truth. *Logismoi* can be defined as thoughts that are intended to distract or disrupt a person (although *logismoi* can also be divinely inspired thoughts as well). The disciplines developed by the Church over the centuries—such as prayer, fasting, and the sacramental life—are intended to purify the *nous* and thus keep our focus on God.

7. Sacrifice
Chess: Sometimes it is wiser to sacrifice a piece early in the game in order to receive a greater benefit later; an exchange of pieces may not be a sacrifice, but an investment.
Christianity: For the uninitiated Christian, fasting is often seen as a punishment or as an exercise in masochism. Yet this type of sacrifice leads to spiritual strength, a self-emptying that allows the Holy Spirit to work within us. The Greek word for "sacrifice," *thysia*, denotes an act of offering, best illustrated in the sacrifice of Christ on the cross. The disciplines

of the Orthodox spiritual life allow for growth and the fulfilling of our potential.

8. Repetition/Practice/Study

Chess: Repetition brings familiarity; study the games of top players and imitate them.

Christianity: The rhythm of the Church calendar helps us to experience the life of Christ repeatedly. The flow of feast and fast periods brings a familiarity and consistency of faith for the practicing Christian. Reading the lives of saints helps us emulate their approach to faith.

9. A Teacher/Guide Is Essential

Chess: A good mentor will help to improve your knowledge and approach to the game.

Christianity: Receiving encouragement and insight from a mature Christian can be fruitful. The Orthodox faith has a long history of spiritual fathers and mothers who offer wisdom and compassion in shepherding the flock. In his book *Inner Way: Toward a Rebirth of Eastern Christian Spiritual Direction*, Joseph Allen offers a concise description of this relationship:

> The spiritual director is like a "literary critic" who, through a relationship of intimacy and trust, helps another Christian to "write" his or her life story. This he does by delving into the various chapters which are already "written," while never neglecting the unfolding present story. This, in turn, equips him to help the directee, by God's grace and that person's own goodwill, to write the continually unfolding future chapters—all, of course, in an atmosphere of sincere prayer.[51]

10. Use Time Wisely

Chess: A chess match is played under very precise time limitations; learn to use your time wisely.

Christianity: Many biblical passages point to the brevity of life: "As for mortals, their days are like grass; they flourish like a flower of the field; for the wind passes over it, and it is gone, and its place knows it no more" (Ps 103:15–16). More importantly, Scripture highlights the urgency of preparing our soul for judgment. In the Gospel of Luke, Jesus offers the Parable of the Rich Man, who tears down his barns in order to build larger ones. God, however, calls him a fool for caring only for his own comfort: "'You fool! This very night your life is being demanded of you. And the things you have prepared, whose will they be?' So it is with those who store up treasures for themselves but are not rich towards God" (Luke 12:20–21). As we can see, God calls the rich man a fool for the limited time he spent cultivating his soul.

There is, of course, a major difference between chess and the spiritual life of a Christian. Chess is a game—but our souls are everything. Just as Jesus used parables and examples from everyday life as a means to reach his audience, I have attempted to make a relevant connection between chess and the spiritual life. Chess champions are single-minded in their pursuit for excellence at chess; Christians have a higher calling.

Listen to these words from Elder Porphyrios, a twentieth-century Orthodox monastic, who offers wisdom to those who are serious about their Christian faith:

> What is holy and beautiful and what gladdens the heart and frees the soul from every evil is the effort to unite yourself to Christ, to love Christ, to crave for Christ and to live in Christ, just as St. Paul said, *It is no longer I who live but Christ who lives in me* (Gal. 2:20). This should be your aim . . . Your most intense effort should be how you will encounter Christ, how you will be united to Him and how you will keep Him in your heart.[52]

WEDDING SERMONS

WHO'S THE BOSS?

The biblical passage read at the sacrament of marriage is from St. Paul's letter to the Ephesians. In the fifth chapter of this Epistle, St. Paul encourages married couples with advice on how to establish a Christian household. After perusing this passage, the contemporary reader ordinarily recoils out of political correctness, citing the seemingly misogynist stand taken by the author. Verses 22 and 23 suggest that the woman should play a subordinate role to the husband in the newly blessed marriage: "Wives, be subject to your husbands as you are to the Lord. For the husband is the head of the wife just as Christ is the head of the church."

The image and language offered in this verse are quickly rejected in our modern age. Critics point out that St. Paul's words are anachronistic, intended for another time and place. Surely the enlightened people of the present century would emphasize egalitarianism and equality within a marriage.

While armchair theologians enjoy referring to the two verses cited above as proof that the Church is out of touch, these same weekend scholars fail to read the verses just before and just after the disputed passage:

Be subject to one another out of reverence for Christ. (v. 21)

Husbands, love your wives, just as Christ loved the church and gave himself up for her. (v. 25)

A closer look at the entire section reveals that St. Paul is fostering mutual sacrifice and surrender, which can only be discovered in an intimate relationship such as marriage. The kind of submission to which St. Paul refers is not one sided, coercive, or dominating. Rather, the mutual compliance that he models is voluntary, subtle, and whole.

Consider the example that St. Paul uses to illustrate the extent of a husband's required commitment to his wife: that of Christ and the Church. This challenge is not for the faint of heart. There is nothing here about the man being the "breadwinner" or the "protector." Instead, St. Paul demands of the husband an ultimate commitment to his wife, a commitment that is equal to Christ's commitment on the cross—one that extends to the point of death! And, like those of Christ, this submission and sacrifice must be offered willingly and joyfully.

What I would also emphasize about these biblical passages is that St. Paul's words to husbands and wives were revolutionary for that era. In those times, women were not legally recognized. They were ill treated and viewed as second-class citizens. For St. Paul to raise the status of women, demanding that husbands love their wives as Christ loved the Church, was compelling and radical.

Although the struggle for women's rights began only about a hundred years ago, in the form of women's suffrage and the Equal Rights Amendment, the Church first established the proper identity and personhood of women from the days of St. Paul the Apostle. But rather than establish a war between the sexes, based on power and control, Paul's words demonstrate mutual support, allegiance, and love.

So what can we ultimately learn from this passage in Ephesians? First, Paul is clearly not derogatory toward women in the context of marriage. Equally, he does not suggest that men should be dominating or self-serving in the marriage relationship. Rather, St. Paul depicts marriage as two souls supporting one another as they strive together for the kingdom of heaven.

THE THREE GIFTS OF MARRIAGE

Joseph and Barbara, we congratulate you on this day of your wedding. Many family and friends are present in this church today to honor you, to pray for you, and to inspire you to live a long and joyous life together. I have been married for fifteen years and continue to learn new things about this holy union. In fact, last week I read an article on marriage that made a great impression on me, and I'd like to share some excerpts with you today.

There was a couple that was celebrating fifty years of marriage. At this golden celebration the invited guests enjoyed dinner, music, dancing, many toasts, and memories. Finally the honored couple was interviewed by the master of ceremonies on stage before bright lights, flash bulbs popping, and video cameras rolling.

"How do you account for such a long and happy marriage?" asked the master of ceremonies. The couple gazed into each other's eyes, smiled, and the old man continued softly, "There are no magic tricks to a long marriage. It's hard work, perseverance, you know—all the things you need to succeed in anything."

After a smattering of applause, the woman, named Irene, carefully took the microphone in her hands and offered a more detailed lesson for all in attendance. "I believe that there are three keys to a successful marriage. The husband and wife must be able to say three important phrases to each other with great frequency: 'I'm sorry,' 'thank you,' and 'I love you.'"

There was complete silence in the reception room as she continued her wise counsel: "There were many times that Jack and I fought, disagreed, whatever, over the years. But we would not give up. We always found it in our hearts to say, 'I'm sorry I hurt you.' We might have had a good cry after that, but forgiving each other made all things new."

Tears began to roll down the faces of people as they sat at the edge of their seats listening to Irene. "The second important phrase that we repeated often over the years was, 'thank you.' For all you young couples here tonight, never take your spouse for granted. If he or she brings you a cup of tea or does your chores for you, say 'thanks.' Appreciate all the little things that the other person does for you."

Irene changed positions on her chair, took a sip of water, and continued her lesson. "And finally, tell your spouse that you love them. Not once or twice or during the first year of marriage—I mean repeatedly, day in and day out. Love is what brought you to the altar; love is what will sustain you; love is the gift that God bestows upon the world."

Irene later apologized for "preaching" to the audience, yet her contribution that evening on the fruit of marriage was the most profound gift that anyone could have shared. The words of Jack and Irene's story ring true because they were spoken by people who prospered in marriage. We can only benefit from their wisdom and experience.

Joseph and Barbara, as you exit the church sanctuary today, may you be inspired and guided by the words of this venerable couple. Go in peace.

THE WEDDING SACRIFICE

Anthony and Sarah, we congratulate and celebrate with you on this day of your wedding. The Orthodox wedding service that you participated in is replete with many symbols and ancient rituals. The rings that you were blessed with represent your commitment to each other. The candles that you held during the service call to mind the light of Christ that will illumine your lives as you journey toward the kingdom of heaven together. The common cup symbolized the joys and sorrows that you will share in this temporal life.

But the symbol that is most impressive is that of the crowns which were placed on your heads. This ritual, which dates back to at least the fourth century, emphasizes two spiritual truths. First, the crowns represent that you have left your families of origin and will now begin your lives together as the king and queen of your new home. It is a definitive statement that you will now establish your own household, with all the responsibilities and blessings which that entails.

More importantly, the crowns symbolize martyrdom. Up to this point in your lives, you most likely lived according to your own will or your own concerns. By entering Christian marriage, you now gladly place aside your personal needs for the benefit of the other person, for the good of the marital union.

The martyrs of the Church clearly understood the reality of sacrifice. When the martyrs were threatened to the point of death, they joyfully sacrificed their lives for the love of Christ. There was little apprehension on their part. There was no resentment or complaining due to their lot in life. They willingly chose to accept martyrdom because of their complete devotion and love for Christ. In a similar manner, by wearing the crowns, you are choosing to sacrifice your own will, gladly and willingly, for your spouse.

The symbolism of martyrdom does not end there. Two of the hymns that are chanted as you process around the table also reflect the image of martyrdom:

O holy martyrs, who fought the good fight and received the crown: entreat the Lord to show mercy on our souls.

Glory to you, Christ God, pride of the Apostles, joy to the martyrs; their proclamation, the Trinity indivisible.

The symbolism of martyrdom in the marriage sacrament may seem odd, even eerie. Yet the Church declares in her teachings that love requires sacrifice, just as Christ suffered crucifixion on our behalf. Sacrificing for others directs us away from self-centeredness, or egoism, and toward sharing, intimacy, and unity. Thus, in the Christian context, sacrifice and martyrdom are not themes of pessimism, but rich soil for growth and fruit-bearing.

May the example of Christ and the martyrs of the Church present an image of hope, joy, and love in your marriage.

EULOGIES

A SAINTLY LIFE

The first few verses of Psalm 13 read as follows:

How long, O Lord? Will you forget me forever? How long will you hide your face from me? How long must I bear pain in my soul, and have sorrow in my heart all day long? (vv. 1–2)

These words were the expression of a person experiencing doubt, anguish, and pain. These words could have so easily been uttered by Helen Thompson, whom we honor today. Due to her sudden illness, she suffered physically, and perhaps emotionally and spiritually, these past few months. It would have been completely understandable for her to cry out, "Where are you, God? Who are you, God?"

We may all be posing those same questions in relation to Helen's death, and it is acceptable to ask such questions. That is the point where true faith begins—with dialogue, even painful dialogue, with God. Our Christian faith permits us to experience spiritual distress and to express it. In the Scripture reading offered earlier, the author felt free to cry out to God, venting all his deeply seated emotions. Sharing with God our inner pain is a positive step toward spiritual healing and wholeness.

Today also brings us an opportunity to rejoice in the inspiring and faithful life of Helen Thompson. The impact that Helen had on our parish community, in only six short years, is remarkable. Helen immersed herself in numerous ministries, using her time and talent to praise God and serve others. She was progressive and fearless when it came to implementing new ideas in the four cornerstones of parish life: worship, fellowship, service, and witness.

We often look to the saints of our Church as examples and role models for how to live a Christian life. May I be bold enough to compare Helen to the list of holy people who have glorified God from generation to generation?

Like St. Katherine, Helen was intelligent and sought to learn more and more about the Christian faith through spiritual reading, study groups, and dialogues about the faith.

Like St. Basil, Helen sought to bring healing and hope to the people who were hungry and homeless.

Like St. Peter, Helen was strong willed and unyielding in living out her faith for herself and for her family.

Like St. Monica, the mother of St. Augustine, Helen instilled the Christian faith in her children, Martin and Demetri, praying for them without fail.

Like St. John of Damascus, Helen saw the hymns of the Church as a way to glorify God through worship.

Like the Virgin Mary, she brought hope to the hopeless and faith to the faithless.

Like St. John the Baptist in John 3:30 ("He must become greater; I must become less"), Helen knew when to be bold and when to be humble and accepting.

And like the Archangel Gabriel, Helen came into our lives to deliver an important message—God is with us.

Although today is filled with much grief, we are not left without hope and comfort. In Psalm 13, the reading I began with, despite very intense questioning of God, the author closes his poetic writing with the following verses:

> But I trusted in your steadfast love; my heart shall rejoice in your salvation. I will sing to the Lord, because he has dealt bountifully with me. (vv. 5–6)

You see, the author of Psalm 13 trusted in God, even in the midst of pain and sorrow. He could do so because he had a dynamic and sustaining relationship with God. Like Helen, the author of Psalm 13 sought to be in communion with our Creator in this life and in the life to come. Helen accepted that the kingdom of heaven begins here and now, even in this fallen world, where we sometimes experience suffering and loss.

St. Cyprian of Carthage, a hierarch of the third century, summarized the Christian's approach to death when he wrote,

> We can think of paradise as being like our native land . . . It is a large and loving community that is waiting for us there: parents, brothers, children, a great and varied gathering who long for us . . . What gladness there shall be both for them and for us, when we enter their presence and their embrace! How sweet are the heavenly realms where death can never terrify us, and life can never end![53]

May her memory be eternal.

THE GREAT COMMANDMENT

There is a narrative found in the Gospel of Matthew that is often said to contain the most powerful words in the New Testament. In this passage, Jesus describes the events of the Great Judgment. We read that Jesus will sit on his glorious throne, with all the angels surrounding him. Before Jesus, all the people throughout history will be gathered, and he will separate them one from another, as a shepherd separates the sheep from the goats. Listen to the words offered by Jesus:

> Then the king will say to those at his right hand, "Come, you that are blessed by my Father, inherit the kingdom prepared for you from the foundation of the world; for I was hungry and you gave me food, I was thirsty and you gave me something to drink, I was a stranger and you welcomed me, I was naked and you gave me clothing, I was sick and you took care of me, I was in prison and you visited me." Then the righteous will answer him, "Lord, when was it that we saw you hungry and gave you food, or thirsty and gave you something to drink? And when was it that we saw you a stranger and welcomed you, or naked and gave you clothing? And when was it that we saw you sick or in prison and visited you?" And the king will answer them, "Truly I tell you, just as you did it to one of the least of these who are members of my family, you did it to me." (Matt 25:34–40)

In this passage, Jesus makes clear that our salvation depends on the care and concern we have for others. This narrative beautifully describes the character of John Smith, whose memory we honor today. John fulfilled this Gospel command by serving others, bringing comfort and hope to those in need. John did not simply satisfy Jesus's command in his spare time. Instead, serving was his vocation, his passion, his essence. The role call of organizations where John volunteered reads like a "Who's Who" of Lancaster charities: the Red Cross of Lancaster General Hospital, the Water Street Rescue Mission, Hospice of Lancaster, and Sertoma of Lancaster. He also served as a teacher's assistant at the Martin Luther King School and in many capacities here at Annunciation Church.

Listing these organizations where John volunteered his time and love would make him quite uncomfortable. This highlights another virtue that made John so special: his humility. A careful reading of this passage from Matthew's Gospel illustrates that the people who were welcomed in the kingdom of heaven were surprised by Jesus's invitation. They did not think of their actions as extraordinary; they simply did what was right, without drawing any attention to themselves. John possessed that same attitude. He was a man of honor and duty who did what was right. No accolades, no banquets, no fame or riches—he simply responded to a call to serve.

Time prevents us from elaborating on other aspects of John's life: his devotion to his loving wife Sarah, the wisdom and example he gave to his children and grandchildren, his work ethic, his more than thirty years of dedicated stewardship at the parish bazaar (which still is manned by the Smith family), and his faithful attendance at worship services here at Annunciation Church.

But there is one more quality that John exuded that demands our attention this morning, and that is his positive attitude. These past few years, John suffered from a series of health issues. Regardless of the obstacles he faced, John's response was always, "We're gonna beat this thing." He had heart surgery, "We're gonna beat this thing." Shingles, "We're gonna beat this thing."

And you know what? John did beat it, because his illnesses were temporary. But his attitude and his disposition and his soul are eternal.

Allow me to close with an excerpt from the writings of Mother Teresa of Calcutta, words with which John would resonate:

> At the end of our lives, we will not be judged by how many diplomas we have received, how much money we have made or how many great things we have done. We will be judged by, "I was hungry and you gave me to eat. I was naked and you clothed me. I was homeless and you took me in."
>
> Hungry not only for bread—but hungry for love.
>
> Naked not only for clothing—but naked of human dignity and respect.
>
> Homeless not only for want of a room of bricks—but homeless because of rejection.
>
> This is Christ in distressing disguise.[54]

THE VIRTUE OF MEEKNESS

One of the most well-known passages from Scripture is called the Beatitudes. In the Beatitudes of the Gospel of Matthew, Jesus offers us nuggets of wisdom on how to live the Christian life. A few prudent items on this list include:

Blessed are the poor in spirit, for theirs is the kingdom of heaven.
Blessed are those who mourn, for they will be comforted.
Blessed are the pure in heart, for they will see God.
(Matt 5:3–4, 8)

Also contained in the Beatitudes is this verse, which beautifully describes Maria, whom we honor today: "Blessed are the meek, for they will inherit the earth" (5:5).

Let me share with you the precise understanding of the word *meek*. Unfortunately, meek is usually associated with *weak*, but cowardice has nothing to do with meekness. Instead, meekness means showing patience and humility, with gentleness. Understood biblically, meekness means making choices and exercising power with a divine, rather than a social, reference point. Meekness is one of the principal attributes of Jesus Christ. He who calls the universe into being, who walks on water, and brings the dead back to life, says of himself, "I am meek and lowly in heart" (Matt 11:29 KJV).

Maria Pappas was born to immigrant parents in Wilmington, Delaware, the second of three children. She graduated high school near the top of her class but lived in an age in which women were not encouraged to fulfill their academic potential. She worked as a physician's secretary until meeting her husband Michael in the early 1950s.

They married and soon after moved to New York City, where they lived for the next twenty-five years. Michael was employed in the shipping industry, which required him to live in New York, the central port in the United States at that time. Although Michael and Maria did not complain openly, the pair, nonetheless, was not enthusiastic about living in New York City. Michael was from a simple European island and Maria from a small city. Thus, New York was a huge adjustment for both of them. But, being dutiful and responsible people, they accepted their circumstances.

It was during this time in New York that Maria fully exhibited the virtue of meekness. Because Michael traveled extensively, Maria was primarily responsible for guiding her two sons through the tumultuous period of the 1960s, not to mention all the distractions and minefields that New York City can thrust upon a family. Yet through her gentle strength, her steadfast spirit, and her humility, Maria succeeded in raising her family with quiet grace.

The members of Maria's family rarely heard her speak ill of others, never heard her use foul language, and not once did she boast or brag about her gifts. In this world, in which we often insist on calling attention to ourselves, Maria always diverted the spotlight onto others.

Many of you have heartfelt memories of Maria. It is important to share these treasures with each other during this time of grief and reflection. This morning I have three such recollections that highlight the depth and breadth of her personality.

First was Maria's intelligence. She would often watch *Jeopardy* with her children and other family members. Maria was quick to respond to the game show questions, which covered a variety of subjects. She was never intimidated when playing Scrabble, Trivial Pursuit, and other board games with her more educated sons. She was always a worthy competitor, displaying her quick recall and intellect.

Second were her navigational skills. Maria was exceptional at reading maps and driving in any circumstance. Whether it was finding a difficult location in New York through rush-hour traffic or chauffeuring her sons to a remote Boy Scout camp site in the dark, Maria was unflappable when it came to navigation.

Third was her selflessness. Maria always considered the needs of others around her before fulfilling her own goals and dreams. She made sure that her husband, her children, and her parents were cared for and content, without voicing any complaint about her own unmet needs. It was only after her parents died and her children were grown that she began exploring her own interests, like learning to play the piano and volunteering her time to various charities. Whatever the circumstance, she adapted to meet the needs of her family, always giving of herself.

We began this morning by highlighting the Beatitudes, especially the verse that instructs us, "Blessed are the meek, for they will inherit the earth" (Matt 5:5). Inheritance, as understood in the court of law, has to do with the distribution of property to the living after someone has died.

But in a biblical context it means receiving all that God has promised. What God promises belongs to the heirs of God—heirs not by birth, but by choice, love, and obedience. May Maria be welcomed into the kingdom of heaven, receiving her inheritance as a faithful child of God. Amen.

THE TEACHER

J esus is referred to by many names in Scripture. He is called the Good Shepherd, Savior, Son of God, and many other titles. But the one name that is most often used in addressing Jesus is *rabbi*, or teacher. A teacher is not simply someone who is knowledgeable about a particular topic, but a person who can convey that knowledge. Better yet, a teacher is someone who can change lives by his words and example. That is why Jesus remains the ideal image of a teacher. He changed lives because he lived by the words he preached.

Jesus would use objects from everyday life in order to teach his followers eternal truths. When Jesus taught people about the meaning of death, he used the example of a grain of wheat. He stated, "Unless a grain of wheat falls into the earth and dies, it remains just a single grain; but if it dies, it bears much fruit" (John 12:24). Jesus's point is that when we live a godly life in this world, upon our death we enter into the kingdom of heaven. In other words, in heaven we receive the fruits of our labor from this world. (That is why, to this day, the symbol of *koliva*, or boiled wheat, represents sweet entrance into the kingdom of heaven.) Whether it was preaching the Sermon on the Mount, or using the parables as illustrations, or counseling someone privately, Jesus was the master Teacher.

Today we honor the life of Evangeline Pappas, a humble teacher and servant of our youth. Evangeline was born in Canton, Ohio, but moved to Scranton, Pennsylvania, at a young age. She graduated from Temple University with a degree in elementary education and then spent almost thirty years of her life teaching in Lancaster-area schools. It is interesting to note that at one time, all four members of the Pappas household were in the public school system at the same time: Evangeline teaching at Butler Elementary School, Thomas teaching at Johnson High School, and their two daughters attending school locally. Education and learning obviously played a large role in the Pappas home.

Evangeline's service to the community did not end with her teaching. She was a faithful volunteer with many organizations, most especially with our own St. Nicholas parish. Our long-time secretary, Cathy Fortner, often spoke of the diligent and reliable work offered by

Evangeline over the course of many years. Cathy commented on Evangeline's gentleness, friendliness, and the quiet style that she exuded.

Evangeline was a proud mother and grandmother, but it was her fifty-two-year marriage to Thomas that deserves our warmest appreciation. On their fiftieth anniversary, a wonderful article was written in the *Scranton Times* on the secret of their marital success. But as Thomas—ever the teacher—pointed out, "There are no secrets." He stated, "A better way to word that is: 'To what do you attribute a happy marriage?'" Thomas and Evangeline then listed twenty-three things that create a healthy marriage. Included in that article are excerpts of a beautiful poem written by Thomas that I hope will be made available to all here present.

On the day of Ascension, when Jesus returned to the kingdom of heaven, he—ever the good teacher—reminded his apostles that he must depart so that the Comforter, the Holy Spirit, could be given to them. Jesus promised the apostles that the Holy Spirit would lead them and guide them to great things, and furthermore that the Holy Spirit would provide them peace and tranquility, even in the midst of difficulties. Today, our community prays that this same Holy Spirit, the Comforter, provide peace and tranquility to the Pappas family. May the servant of God Evangeline be welcomed into the kingdom of heaven. May her memory be eternal. Amen.

A SERVANT OF GOD

Just before his arrest and Crucifixion, Jesus met with the twelve apostles to offer them an essential spiritual lesson. He had taught his followers many things over the prior three years, but this final teaching was the cornerstone of the gospel message. In the upper room, following the institution of the Lord's Supper, Jesus got up from the table, took off his outer robe, and tied a towel around his waist. Then he poured water into a basin and began to wash the disciples' feet and to wipe them with the towel that was tied around him. After he had washed their feet, he put on his robe and returned to the table. Jesus said to them, "Do you know what I have done to you? You call me Teacher and Lord—and you are right, for that is what I am. So if I, your Lord and Teacher, have washed your feet, you also ought to wash one another's feet. For I have set you an example, that you also should do as I have done to you" (John 13:12–15). The final lesson that Jesus conveyed to his apostles was the command to humbly serve others.

Maria Pappas, whom we honor today, was a servant. She followed the example of servanthood as modeled by Jesus. From an early age she was placed in positions of responsibility that demanded maturity, discipline, and hard work. Maria's mother, Janet, worked two menial jobs in order to support the family. Because Janet could not care for the two youngest children, Maria stepped forward to raise her sisters Connie and Gertrude.

Decades later, Maria became a parent herself, selflessly tending the needs of her own husband and children. When her sons, Michael and Thomas, needed encouragement and direction, it was Maria who provided strong guidance and steadfast loyalty.

Maria and her husband, Matthew, owned and operated a small but successful restaurant downtown. When someone entered Theo's Café and wanted to be served a delicious meal, it was Maria Pappas who did the serving. In all things, Maria looked to serve and fulfill the needs of others.

Maria was a simple woman, unselfish and easily contented. She rarely complained about her life's circumstances. Although she never traveled farther east than Wildwood, New Jersey, or farther west than her native West Virginia, she emboldened her sons to reach for the stars. She imparted to them a strong work ethic and respect for others, virtues that she modeled in her own life.

There was also a soft side to Maria that we should call to mind today. She was a terrific cook, passing along recipes to her posterity. Together with her Matthew, Maria was a great dancer, reveling in the ethnic and modern dances of the times. She was active at St. Nicholas Church and spoke at length with her children and grandchildren about her relationship with Christ.

The legacy that Maria leaves is not irrelevant to us here today. Her true legacy is a challenge to each person in this sanctuary—a call to action today and into the future. Just as Jesus washed the apostles' feet, inspiring them to be servants, Maria is extolling each of us to follow her example of servanthood. Jesus reminds us that "whoever wishes to be great among you must be your servant" (Matt 20:26). Maria Pappas followed that axiom all her life. May her memory be eternal. Amen.

NOTES

Part One: Development of Preaching in the Orthodox Church

1. Joseph J. Allen, *The Ministry of the Church: Image of Pastoral Care* (Crestwood, NY: St. Vladimir's Seminary Press, 1986), 129.

2. David Dunn-Wilson, *A Mirror for the Church: Preaching in the First Five Centuries* (Grand Rapids, MI: Eerdmans, 2005), xv.

3. Ibid., 3.

4. Ibid., 11.

5. Allen, *Ministry of the Church*, 140.

6. Paul S. Wilson, *A Concise History of Preaching* (Nashville: Abingdon, 1992), 25.

7. Michael H. Holmes, *Apostolic Fathers in English* (Grand Rapids, MI: Baker Academic, 2006), 23.

8. Ibid., 42.

9. Ibid., 106.

10. Ibid., 114.

11. Ibid., 296.

12. Justin Martyr, *First Apology* 6, in *The Fathers of the Church: Writings of St. Justin Martyr*, trans. Thomas B. Falls (New York: Christian Heritage, Inc., 1948), 38–39.

13. L. Mattei, *Philosophy and Early Christianity* (Nairobi: Consolata Press, 1995), 91ff.

14. Justin Martyr, *Second Apology* 10, in *Fathers of the Church*, 129.

15. Clement of Alexandria, *Christ the Educator*, trans. Simon P. Wood, vol. 23 of The Fathers of the Church (New York: Fathers of the Church, Inc., 1954), 48.

16. Alexander Olivar, "Reflections on Problems Raised by Early Christian Preaching," 21–32, in *Preacher and Audience: Studies in Early Christian and Byzantine Homiletics*, eds. Mary B. Cunningham and Pauline Allen (Leiden, Netherlands: Brill, 1998), 23.

17. Georges Florovsky, *The Eastern Fathers of the Fourth Century*, vol. 7 of The Collected Works of Georges Florovsky (Vaduz, Germany: Büchervertriebsanstalt, 1987), 72–75.

18. Basil the Great, *On the Holy Spirit* (Crestwood, NY: St. Vladimir's Seminary Press, 1980), 59.

19. Allen, *Ministry of the Church*, 144.

20. Ibid., 145.

21. Basil the Great, *St. Basil: Exegetic Homilies*, vol. 46 of The Fathers of the Church (Washington, DC: Catholic University of America Press, 1981), 151.

22. Anthony Meredith, *The Cappadocians* (Crestwood, NY: St. Vladimir's Seminary Press, 1995), 35.

23. Florovsky, *Eastern Fathers of the Fourth Century*, 112.

24. Meredith, *Cappadocians*, 46.

25. Gregory of Nazianzus, *Oration* 29.19–20, in Meredith, *Cappadocians*, 308–9.

26. Gregory of Nazianzus, *Apologia* 71, in Meredith, *Cappadocians*, 338.

27. Dunn-Wilson, *Mirror for the Church*, 107.

28. Ibid.

29. J. N. D. Kelly, *Golden Mouth: The Story of John Chrysostom* (London: Duckworth, 1995), in Dunn-Wilson, *Mirror for the Church*, 107.

30. Allen, *Ministry of the Church*, 147.

31. Ibid.

32. Ibid., 147.

33. John Chrysostom, *Homily 9 on Romans 4:23*, 1.4.25, in vol. 11 of Nicene and Post-Nicene Fathers, Schaff, ed., First Series (1851; repr., Grand Rapids, MI: Eerdmans, 1979), 396.

34. Chrysostom, *Homily* 1.9, in *Homilies on Genesis*, vol. 74 of The Fathers of the Church (Washington, DC: Catholic University of America Press, 1985), 26.

35. Chrysostom, *Homily 4*, in *Commentary on St. John the Apostle and Evangelist*, vol. 33 of The Fathers of the Church (New York: Fathers of the Church, Inc., 1957), 46.

36. Chrysostom, in book 5 of *Six Books on the Priesthood*, trans. Graham Neville (Crestwood, NY: St. Vladimir's Seminary Press, 1984), 72.

37. Ibid., 71.

38. Andrew Louth, "St. John Damascene: Preacher and Poet," in *Preacher and Audience: Studies in Early Christian and Byzantine Homiletics*, ed. Mary B. Cunningham and Pauline Allen (Leiden, Netherlands: Brill, 1998), 251.

39. Ibid., 255.

40. John of Damascus, *Three Treatises on the Divine Images* (henceforth *On the Divine Images*), trans. Andrew Louth (Crestwood, NY: St. Vladimir's Seminary Press, 1980), 23.

41. John of Damascus, *Homily* 1.16, in *On the Divine Images*, 23.

42. "From the Life of St. Gregory Palamas, Archbishop, Miracle-Worker of Thessalonika: How All Christians in General Must Pray without Ceasing," in *Early Fathers from the Philokalia*, trans. E. Kadloubovsky and G. E. H. Palmer (London: Faber and Faber, 1954), 413–14.

43. Gregory Palamas, *Homily on the Annunciation*, in *The Homilies of St. Gregory Palamas*, ed. Christopher Veniamin (South Canaan, PA: St. Tikhon's Seminary Press, 2002), 166.

44. Nomikos M. Vaporis, *Father Kosmas: The Apostle of the Poor* (Brookline, MA: Holy Cross Orthodox Press, 1977), 15.

45. Ibid., 10.

46. Ibid., 53.

47. Ibid., 1.

48. Allen, *Ministry of the Church*, 158.

49. Ibid., 161.

Part Two: Selected Sermons

1. Christopher Hitchens, *God is Not Great: How Religion Poisons Everything* (New York: Twelve, 1999), 4.

2. Patriarch Bartholomew, "Our Invisible Environment," *Wall Street Journal*, October 26, 2009.

3. H. Skolimowski, "Eco-Ethics as the Imperative of Our Times," *Epiphany Journal*, Spring 1983.

4. Alice Gray, *Stories of the Heart* (Sisters, OR: Multnomah Books, 1996), 27.

5. Alexander Schmemann, *The Eucharist: Sacrament of the Kingdom*, trans. Paul Kachur (Crestwood, NY: St. Vladimir's Seminary Press, 1987), 245.

6. Anthony 6, in Benedicta Ward, trans., *Sayings of the Desert Fathers: The Alphabetical Collection* (London: A. R. Mobray & Co.; Kalamazoo, MI: Cistercian Publications, 1975), 2.

7. Anthony 16, in Ward, *Sayings of the Desert Fathers*, 3.

8. Helen Waddell, *The Desert Fathers: Translations from the Latin* (New York: Vintage Books, 1998), 69.

9. Anthony 3, in Ward, *Sayings of the Desert Fathers*, 2.

10. Mother Teresa, *Mother Teresa: Come Be My Light; The Private Writings of the Saint of Calcutta*, ed. Brian Kolodiejchuk (New York: Doubleday, 1997), 288.

11. Mother Teresa, *Come Be My Light*, 187.

12. John of Kronstadt, *Spiritual Counsels: Select Passages from* My Life in Christ, ed. W. Jardine Grisbrooke (Crestwood, NY: St. Vladimir's Seminary Press, 1967), 216–17.

13. *Merriam Webster's Collegiate Dictionary*, 11th ed., s.v. "Astrology."

14. Alexander Karloutsos, "Astrology is Astrolatry," Greek Orthodox Archdiocese of America, http://www.goarch.org/ourfaith/ourfaith7066.

15. Karloutsos, "Astrology is Astrolatry."

16. Anthony de Mello, *The Song of the Bird* (New York, NY: Doubleday Books, 1982), 77.

17. Jim Forest, *The Ladder of the Beatitudes* (Maryknoll, NY: Orbis Books, 2000), 41–42.

18. Frank Schaeffer and John Schaeffer, *Keeping Faith* (New York: Carrol & Graf Publishers, 2002), 45.

19. Ibid., 72.

20. Ibid., 184–85.

21. C. S. Lewis, *Mere Christianity* (New York: HarperSanFrancisco, 2001), 52.

22. de Mello, *The Song of the Bird*, 153.

23. John of Kronstadt, *Spiritual Counsels*, 17.

24. Erma Bombeck, "When God Created Mothers," syndicated column, May 12, 1974.

25. John A. Logan, *General Order No. 11*, issued from Headquarters of the Grand Army of the Republic, Washington, DC, May 5, 1868. Online at Sons of Union Veterans of the Civil War National Headquarters, http://www.suvcw.org/logan.htm.

26. John of Kronstadt, *Spiritual Counsels*, 96.

27. Stuart Hample and Eric Marshall, *Children's Letters to God: The New Collection*, illustrated by Tom Bloom (New York: Workman Publishing, 1991).

28. Note to preacher: Few parishioners are well versed in the timeline of Church history. Yet with the plethora of Christian churches dotting the landscape, the Orthodox faithful need to be exposed to fundamental events from apostolic times to the present. The outline can be inserted in the weekly bulletin and elaborated upon either in one sermon presentation or two.

29. Raymo, "It All Adds up to a Very Big Bang," *Boston Globe*, May 27, 1996.

30. Stephen Jay Gould, "Evolution as Fact and Theory," *Discover* 2, no. 5 (1981): 34–37.

31. *Mere Christianity*, 115.

32. Corrie ten Boom, *Tramp for the Lord* (New York: Jove Books, 1974), 55.

33. Anthony Bloom, *Meditations on a Theme: A Spiritual Journey* (London: Continuum, 2003), 105.

34. Evagrius Ponticus, *The Praktikos: Chapters on Prayer*, trans. John Bamberger (Spencer, MA: Cistercian Publications, 1970), in Roberta C. Bondi, *To*

Pray & to Love: Conversations on Prayer with the Early Church (Minneapolis: Augsburg Fortress, 1991), 113.

35. Note to preacher: The quotes provided here can be used as a teaching tool by including them as an insert in your weekly bulletin and by elaborating upon several of the quotes in your presentation. Develop the theme and application of each quote.

36. *Unseen Warfare*, ed. Nicodemus of the Holy Mountain, trans. E. Kadloubovsky and G. E. H. Palmer (Crestwood, NY: St. Vladimir's Seminary Press, 1987), 72.

37. Ibid., 250.

38. Ibid., 183.

39. Ibid., 176.

40. Ibid., 266.

41. Ibid., 206.

42. Ibid., 279.

43. Ibid., 81.

44. Ibid., 181.

45. *Service of the Small Paraklesis to the Most Holy Theotokos*, trans. Kangelaris and Kasemeotes (Brookline, MA: Holy Cross Orthodox Press, 1984), 8.

46. Ibid., 14.

47. Ibid., 13.

48. Ibid.

49. Ibid., 36.

50. Please note: This message is a combination of text and notes. It can be edited based on the speaker's interest and knowledge of chess, and what Christian resources the speaker wants to include.

51. Joseph J. Allen, *Inner Way: Toward a Rebirth of Eastern Christian Spiritual Direction* (Brookline, MA: Holy Cross Orthodox Press, 2000), 6.

52. Elder Porphyrios, *Wounded By Love: The Life and the Wisdom of Elder Porphyrios*, trans. John Raffan (Limni, Evia, Greece: Denise Harvey, 2005), 137–38.

53. Cyprian of Carthage, *Born to New Life*, trans. Tim Witherow (New Rochelle, NY: New City Press, 1992), 115.

54. Mother Teresa, *Works of Love Are Works of Peace: Mother Teresa of Calcutta and the Missionaries of Charity* (San Francisco: Ignatius Press, 1996), 35.

BIBLIOGRAPHY

Allen, Joseph J. *The Ministry of the Church: Image of Pastoral Care*. Crestwood, NY: St. Vladimir's Seminary Press, 1986.

_____. *Inner Way: Toward a Rebirth of Eastern Christian Spiritual Direction*. Brookline, MA: Holy Cross Orthodox Press, 2000.

Basil the Great. *On the Holy Spirit*. Crestwood, NY: St. Vladimir's Seminary Press, 1980.

_____. *St. Basil: Exegetic Homilies*. Vol. 46 of The Fathers of the Church. Washington, DC: Catholic University of America Press, 1981.

Bloom, Anthony. *Meditations on a Theme: A Spiritual Journey*. London: Continuum, 2003. First published by Mowbrays, 1972.

Bombeck, Erma. *When God Created Mothers*. Riverside, NJ: Andrews McMeel Publishing, 2005.

Clement of Alexandria. *Christ the Educator*. Translated by Simon P. Wood. Vol. 23 of The Fathers of the Church. New York: Fathers of the Church, Inc., 1954.

Coniaris, Anthony. *Preaching the Word of God*. Brookline, MA: Holy Cross Orthodox Press, 1983.

Cunningham, Mary B., and Pauline Allen. *Preacher and Audience: Studies in Early Christian and Byzantine Homiletics*. Leiden, Netherlands: Brill, 1998.

Cyprian of Carthage. *Born to New Life*. Translated by Tim Witherow. New Rochelle, NY: New City Press, 1992.

de Mello, Anthony. *The Song of the Bird*. New York, NY: Doubleday Books, 1982.

Dunn-Wilson, David. *A Mirror for the Church: Preaching in the First Five Centuries*. Grand Rapids, MI: Eerdmans, 2005.

Edwards, O. C. *The History of Preaching*. Nashville: Abingdon Press, 2004.

Evagrius Ponticus. *The Praktikos: Chapters on Prayer*. Translated by John Bamberger. Spencer, MA: Cistercian Publications, 1970.

Florovsky, Georges. *The Eastern Fathers of the Fourth Century*. Vol. 7 of The Collected Works of Georges Florovsky. Vaduz, Germany: Büchervertriebsanstalt, 1987.

Forest, Jim. *The Ladder of the Beatitudes*. Maryknoll, NY: Orbis Books, 2000.

Gould, Stephen Jay. "Evolution as Fact and Theory." *Discover* 2, no. 5 (1981): 34–37.

Gray, Alice. *Stories of the Heart*. Sisters, OR: Multnomah Books, 1996.

Hample, Stuart, and Eric Marshall. *Children's Letters to God: The New Collection*. Illustrated by Tom Bloom. New York: Workman Publishing, 1991.

Harakas, Stanley. *The Orthodox Church: 455 Questions & Answers*. Minneapolis, MN: Light & Life Publishing, 1987.

Hitchens, Christopher. *God is Not Great: How Religion Poisons Everything*. New York: Twelve, 1999.

Holmes, Michael H. *Apostolic Fathers in English*. Grand Rapids, MI: Baker Academic, 2006.

John Chrysostom. *Commentary on St. John the Apostle and Evangelist*. Vol. 33 of The Fathers of the Church. New York: Fathers of the Church, Inc., 1957.

———. *Homilies on Genesis*. Vol. 74 of The Fathers of the Church. Washington, DC: Catholic University of America Press, 1985.

———. *Six Books on the Priesthood*. Translated by Graham Neville. Crestwood, NY: St. Vladimir's Seminary Press, 1984.

John of Damascus. *Three Treatises on the Divine Images*. Translated by Andrew Louth. Crestwood, NY: St. Vladimir's Seminary Press, 1980.

John of Kronstadt. *Spiritual Counsels: Select Passages from* My Life in Christ. Edited by W. Jardine Grisbrooke. Crestwood, NY: St. Vladimir's Seminary Press, 1967.

Justin Martyr. *The Fathers of the Church: Writings of St. Justin Martyr*. Translated by Thomas B. Falls. New York: Christian Heritage, Inc., 1948.

Kadloubovsky, E., and G. E. H. Palmer, trans. *Early Fathers from the Philokalia*. London: Faber and Faber, 1954.

Karloutsos, Alexander. "Astrology is Astrolatry." Greek Orthodox Archdiocese of America. http://www.goarch.org/ourfaith/ourfaith7066.

Lewis, C. S. *Mere Christianity*. HarperCollins Edition 2001. New York: HarperSanFrancisco, 2001.

Louth, Andrew. "St. John Damascene: Preacher and Poet." In Cunningham and Allen, *Preacher and Audience*, 247–65.

Mattei, L. *Philosophy and Early Christianity*. Nairobi: Consolata Press, 1995.

Meredith, Anthony. *The Cappadocians.* Crestwood, NY: St. Vladimir's Seminary Press, 1995.

Meyendorff, John. *Marriage: An Orthodox Perspective.* Crestwood, NY: St. Vladimir's Seminary Press, 1984.

Olivar, Alexander. "Reflections on Problems Raised by Early Christian Preaching." In Cunningham and Allen, *Preacher and Audience,* 21–32.

Porphyrios (Elder). *Wounded By Love: The Life and the Wisdom of Elder Porphyrios.* Edited from an archive of notes and recordings by the Sisters of the Holy Convent of Chrysopigi. Translated by John Raffan. Limni, Evia, Greece: Denise Harvey, 2005.

Schaeffer, Frank, and John Schaeffer. *Keeping Faith.* New York: Carrol & Graf Publishers, 2002.

Schaff, Philip, general ed. *Saint Chrysostom: Homilies on the Acts and the Epistle to the Romans.* Vol. 11 of Nicene and Post-Nicene Fathers, First Series. 1851. Reprint, Grand Rapids, MI: Eerdmans, 1979.

Schmemann, Alexander. *The Eucharist: Sacrament of the Kingdom.* Translated by Paul Kachur. Crestwood, NY: St. Vladimir's Seminary Press, 1987.

Service of the Small Paraklesis to the Most Holy Theotokos. Translated and set to meter by Demetri Kangelaris and Nicholas Kasemeotes. Brookline, MA: Holy Cross Orthodox Press, 1984. Revised 1997.

ten Boom, Corrie. *Tramp for the Lord.* New York: Jove Books, 1974.

Teresa (Mother). *Mother Teresa: Come Be My Light; The Private Writings of the Saint of Calcutta.* Edited by Brian Kolodiejchuk. New York: Doubleday, 1997.

———. *Works of Love Are Works of Peace: Mother Teresa of Calcutta and the Missionaries of Charity.* Photographs and introduction by Michael Callopy. San Francisco: Ignatius Press, 1996.

Unseen Warfare. Edited by Nicodemus of the Holy Mountain and translated by E. Kadloubovsky and G. E. H. Palmer. Crestwood, NY: St. Vladimir's Seminary Press, 1987.

Vaporis, Nomikos M. *Father Kosmas: The Apostle of the Poor.* Brookline, MA: Holy Cross Orthodox Press, 1977.

Veniamin, Christopher. *The Homilies of St. Gregory of Palamas.* South Canaan, PA: St. Tikhon's Seminary Press, 2002.

Waddell, Helen. *The Desert Fathers: Translations from the Latin.* New York: Vintage Books, 1998.

Ward, Benedicta, trans. *Sayings of the Desert Fathers: The Alphabetical Collection.* London: A. R. Mobray & Co.; Kalamazoo, MI: Cistercian Publications, 1975.

Wilson, Paul S. *A Concise History of Preaching.* Nashville: Abingdon, 1992.

About the Author

Fr. Alexander Goussetis has served as pastor, university professor, retreat leader, and speaker in his twenty years of ministry. He has authored three previous books, published and distributed by Light & Life Publishing:

- *Renewed Day by Day: An Orthodox Prayer Workbook*–features twenty-eight exercises for learning and developing deeper practices in Orthodox spirituality
- *Encountering World Religions: An Orthodox Christian Perspective*– offers the basic teachings of many of the world religions, with an Orthodox Christian response
- *A Rebel's Journey: A Novel of Doubt & Christian Transformation*– uses a fictional backdrop to engage young adults in searching for the ancient Christian faith

Fr. Goussetis is a former CPA, a graduate of Holy Cross Greek Orthodox School of Theology, and has earned a doctoral degree from Andover Newton Theological School in the field of Psychology and Pastoral Counseling. His pastoral emphasis is making the Orthodox faith relevant to people in their everyday lives, and educating our faithful in articulating the teachings of the Church to others. He currently serves as pastor of Annunciation Greek Orthodox Church, Lancaster, PA.

9 781935 317203